Truly Devoted

H. Norman Wright

HARVEST HOUSE PUBLISHERS
EUGENE, OREGON

Cover photos © 2012, courtesy of Watts Photography, Bakersfield, CA

Cover design by Left Coast Design, Portland, Oregon

The author and Harvest House Publishers have made every effort to trace the ownership of all quotes and stories. In the event of a question arising from the use of a poem, quote, or story, we regret any error made and will be pleased to make the necessary correction in future editions of this book.

TRULY DEVOTED
Copyright © 2013 by H. Norman Wright
Published by Harvest House Publishers
Eugene, Oregon 97402
www.harvesthousepublishers.com

Library of Congress Cataloging-in-Publication Data
    Wright, H. Norman.
    Truly devoted / H. Norman Wright.
        pages cm
    ISBN 978-0-7369-5240-8 (pbk.)
    ISBN 978-0-7369-5241-5 (eBook)
    1. Dog owners—Religious life. 2. Dogs—Religious aspects—Christianity—Meditations. I. Title.
    BV4596.A54W75 2013
    242—dc23

                                        2012047324

Printed in the United States of America

13 14 15 16 17 18 19 20 / BP-JH / 10 9 8 7 6 5 4 3

Greetings

It's been a long day at work. You're looking forward to getting home to your place of refuge. Your mind drifts to a delicious dinner, resting awhile, and all the family members eagerly awaiting your arrival. You pull into the driveway and "accidentally on purpose" hit the horn to let everyone know you're home so they'll come to greet you. A few seconds go by, and no one comes so you get out of the car and stroll to the door. Still no one around.

You go inside and yell, "I'm home!" Silence. One child runs by and mumbles, "Hi, Dad," and keeps on going. You can hear another child in his room judging by the volume of the music. You make your way to the kitchen, expecting dinner to be in progress, but again there are no people around—only a note stating the cook will be late but there's food to put in the microwave.

No one came to greet you. What a letdown! But that doesn't happen to you or me. Why? Yes, you guessed it. We are dog owners! And our pups are always excited to see us. Let's rerun the scenario with them included.

You walk up to the door. What's that sound you hear from inside the house? You tilt your head to hear better. Yes, it's a whine and then a series of barks. The animal on the other side of that door is awaiting your presence. He's so excited to see you! You open the door and there he is. Depending on the breed, the dog may get so excited he piddles on the floor. Or he may run around and around, chasing his tail. Or perhaps he's sitting patiently waiting for a pat on the head. Maybe he's jumping up to lick your face.

Some dogs follow us everywhere we go, while others try to talk to us with their doggy sounds. Some have tails that swish back and forth a mile a minute. Perhaps your dog is trained to bring your slippers to you. Or maybe your dog has OCBD (Obsessive Compulsive Ball Disorder). He brings his tennis ball to you the instant he knows you're coming. I know some dogs who bring their leashes because they want us to walk them. Yes, dogs are wonderful greeters, and we can learn a lot from them.

The Importance of Recognition

We all want to be greeted, welcomed, acknowledged. If we're married, how we greet each other when we meet after an absence is vital. At one of the marriage seminars I conduct, a husband shared, "When I get home at the end of the day, I have to go looking for my wife. She never comes to the door to greet me. I get a better greeting from my dog. He comes running to see me, wags his tail like it's going to fall off, runs around me, licks my hand, and makes little barking sounds."

Before I could respond, another husband piped up. "You want your wife to do all that?"

Soon the entire group was responding to the comment and scenario.

Are you aware that how you and your partner, family members, and even friends greet each other when you first meet at the end of the day sets the tone for the evening? That initial greeting is so critical. The first four minutes establishes the foundation for the rest of the time spent together. If your first contact includes a listing of everything that went wrong during the day, or a list of negatives, or, worse yet, complaints and criticisms of the other person, you can just imagine what the rest of the evening will be like. But if that first contact at the end of the day is similar to the greetings we get from our dogs, what a difference that would make. What if everyone involved was positive and caring and bright during that first four minutes of contact? Later on they could discuss the issues of the day, and everyone would probably be in a better mood and have a better attitude for that process. Yes, dogs model the art of greeting one another joyfully.

One of my favorite authors, Max Lucado, has an interesting story on the impact of how we're greeted when we arrive home. He travels quite a bit, and in *The Applause of Heaven* he describes what happens when he heads home.

> Home. The longest part of going home is the last part—the plane's taxiing to the terminal from the runway. I'm the fellow the flight attendant always has to tell to sit down.
>
> There is a leap of the heart as I exit the plane. I almost get nervous as I walk up the ramp. I step past people. I grip my satchel. My stomach tightens. My palms sweat. I walk into the lobby like an actor walking onto a stage. The curtain is lifted, and the audience stands in a half-moon. Most of the people see that I'm not the one they want and look past me.
>
> But from the side I hear the familiar shriek of two little girls. "Daddy!" I turn and see them—faces scrubbed, standing on chairs, bouncing up and down in joy as the man in their life walks toward them. Jenna stops bouncing just long enough to clap. She applauds![1]

Can you imagine what that must be like? To have a family member *applaud* when she sees you? Dogs don't applaud like we do, but they certainly do it in their special way. Max goes on with his story:

> Faces of home. That is what makes the promise at the end of the Beatitudes so compelling: "Rejoice and be glad, because great is our reward in heaven."
>
> What is our reward? Home.
>
> The book of Revelation could be entitled the book of Homecoming, for in it we are given a picture of our heavenly home.

John's descriptions of the future steal your breath. His description of the final battle is graphic. Good clashes with evil. The sacred encounters the sinful. The pages howl with the shrieks of dragons and smolder with the coals of fiery pits. But in the midst of the battlefield there is a rose. John describes it in chapter 21:

> Then I saw a new heaven and a new earth, for the first heaven and the first earth had passed away, and there was no longer any sea. I saw the Holy City, the new Jerusalem, coming down out of heaven from God, prepared as a bride beautifully dressed for her husband. And I heard a loud voice from the throne saying, "Now the dwelling of God is with men, and he will live with them. They will be his people, and God himself will be with them and be their God. He will wipe every tear from their eyes. There will be no more death or mourning or crying or pain, the old order of things has passed away."
>
> He who was seated on the throne said, "I am making everything new!" (Rev. 21:1-5, NIV).[2]

Max concludes the chapter this way:

> I'll be home soon. My plane is nearing San Antonio. I can feel the nose of the jet dipping downward. I can see the flight attendants getting ready. Denalyn is somewhere in the parking lot, parking the car and hustling the girls toward the terminal.
>
> I'll be home soon. The plane will land. I'll walk down that ramp and hear my name and see their faces. I'll be home soon.
>
> You'll be home soon, too. You may not have noticed it, but you are closer to home than ever before. Each moment is a step taken. Each breath is a page turned. Each day is a mile

marked, a mountain climbed. You are closer to home than you've ever been.

Before you know it, your appointed arrival time will come; you'll descend the ramp and enter the City. You'll see faces that are waiting for you. You'll hear your name spoken by those who love you. And, maybe, just maybe—in the back, behind the crowds—the One who would rather die than live without you will remove his pierced hands from his heavenly robe and…applaud.[3]

Can you imagine? Applause in heaven when you arrive! As I write this devotional, I'm a bit sad this evening. It's August 15, my son Matthew's birthday. He would have been 45 today. He died when he was 22. He was disabled and, although he was that age physically, mentally he was only 18 months old. He was such a blessing, and he changed our lives. When I first read *The Applause of Heaven* and came to this homecoming part, I felt a sense of joy as I realized that when Matthew was called home there was a tremendous round of applause for him in heaven. There will be for you too if you have a personal relationship with Jesus. Dogs greet us. Family and friends greet us. Even strangers greet us. But the ultimate greeting awaits us in heaven.

The Master's Voice

Your voice has a certain ring to it, and so does mine. Some voices are quite distinct. Mothers seem to have a unique ability to hear their children's voices in a room of 20 or more yelling children. In a herd of cows, there might be 50 bawling calves, but each mother cow knows which one is her own. Your dog knows your voice too, and he responds to it. In fact, dogs love to hear their masters' voices. There's a familiarity and sense of comfort in hearing the sound.

There was a Boston terrier by the name of Tad. He was brought into his family when he was three months old, and it didn't take long for everyone to think, and excuse the expression, he was the cat's meow. Tad was adopted when the family was on a trip visiting their daughter Kayla. He loved each family member—but especially Kayla.

The family stayed for their three-week visit, and Tad developed a routine of playing with Kayla before she left for work. He would be waiting at the door each day when she returned home from work.

When the family left with Tad, they let him talk to Kayla on the phone a few times as they drove home. And whenever they called her from their home, they always let their pup talk with her. As many dogs do, when he heard her voice he would listen, cock his head, scratch the phone, and look into it to find her.

One day Kayla called and left a message on the answering machine. When Tad's owner pressed the button to listen to the message, the pup was standing there watching and listening and wagging his tail.

He enjoyed it so much that his master played it again for him. A few days later, his owner was taking a shower when he heard the answering machine turn on. He recognized his daughter's voice leaving a message. He heard the message repeat, and then he heard the machine announce, "End of messages." A few seconds later he heard his daughter's voice again. *How strange*, he thought. His curiosity got the best of him, so he turned off the water, got out of the shower, dried off, threw on a robe, and went quietly into the other room. Tad was standing by the machine listening. When the message was over, he stood up with his front paws on the edge of the low table. Then he slapped the answering machine with a paw. The message came on again! He experienced an immediate, positive reinforcement for his efforts.

His owner watched, and when Tad did it again, his master said, "No, Tad. Bad dog!" Then he pushed the machine's erase button. A few days later he heard a voice from the living room. "You have no messages." Then it played again. "You have no messages." And it played again. He got up to investigate and found Tad by the machine. The dog was upset because every time he tapped the button he heard the machine's voice instead of the message he wanted to hear. He began hitting the machine with both paws. When he was told to stop and leave it alone, he looked at his owner, ignored the command, and increased his efforts to hear the voice he wanted. He then ran back and forth between the machine and his owner, who decided to solve this problem once and for all. Kayla was called and asked to call back and leave Tad a message. When she did, the owner didn't erase it. That way Tad could play the message and listen to the voice whenever he wanted to.

Dogs recognize the voices of their masters! Tad delighted in hearing Kayla's voice more than any other. He could distinguish her voice. In our daily lives, we listen to voice after voice throughout the day. Some we like, some we don't. We even have voices in our heads! Some of them are attached to experiences from our past, good and bad. Sometimes these voices, or old memories, from the past dominate our present. Sometimes we need to press the erase button on the machine that recorded the messages.

We're all influenced by voices from others or from our culture. Some we discard; some we heed. Some we shouldn't follow. There is one voice, however, that we should always listen to, but sometimes we don't hear it or we may even chose to ignore it. It's the voice of our Master. He leaves messages all the time. They come through His Word, through other people, or even silently during our times of reflection:

> The voice of the LORD is over the waters; the God of glory thunders, the LORD thunders over the mighty waters. The voice of the LORD is powerful; the voice of the LORD is majestic. The voice of the LORD breaks the cedars; the LORD breaks in pieces the cedars of Lebanon (Psalm 29:3-5).

> The gatekeeper opens the gate for him, and the sheep listen to his voice. He calls his own sheep by name and leads them out. When he has brought out all his own, he goes on ahead of them, and his sheep follow him because they know his voice (John 10:3-5).

> As has just been said: "Today, if you hear his voice, do not harden your hearts as you did in the rebellion" (Hebrews 3:15).

Some people look forward to hearing God's voice and following it. Others prefer not to or simply tune Him out. The messages keep coming in, but the people never check their messages or go back to the answering machine to hear Him again. God pursues us more than we "scratch and paw" at the answering machine so we can hear His voice. I like how Howard Macy describes God's pursuit of us:

> Those who recall Francis Thompson's haunting image of God as the Hound of Heaven, pursuing us down the halls of time, might well ask who, in fact, is the hound and who

the quarry, whether we seek God or whether we are sought. What we discover is that all the while we have been pursuing God, he has been rushing toward us with reckless love, arms flung wide to hug us home. God aches for every person, for every creature, indeed, for every scrap of life in all creation to be joined again in the unity that was its first destiny. So while we are crying out, "Where are you, God?" the divine voice echoes through our hiding places, "Where are you?" Indeed, the story of the Garden of Eden reminds us that it is God who calls out first, and to this we answer. God's yearning for us stirs up our longing in response. God's initiating presence may be ever so subtle—an inward tug of desire, a more-than-coincidence meeting of words and events, a glimpse of the beyond in a storm or in a flower—but it is enough to make the heart skip a beat and to make us want to know more.[1]

What does the voice of God say to us? "I love you. I want you. I sent My Son for you." Let's listen…listen to the voice of our Master and delight in Him.

Secret Sins of Your Dog

Does your dog ever sin? Of course he does. All dogs do. Oh, you might not call it sin. You may use a nicer word, such as misbehave or disobedient. But sin is sin. Have you ever asked your dog, "Did you take that?" or "Did you eat that?" and then hear a confession or see true remorse in his eyes? "Oh, yes, it's true. I did that. I'm so sorry." Usually they lie themselves out of their responsibility with a puzzled look, or a dumb look, or grovel because of our tone of voice, or ignore us. I know because my dogs have lied to me. Like the times when I'm ready to take them for a walk so I ask if they need to go potty or if they already did. They look at me with an expression that says, "Of course we did. No problem." And 30 feet down the sidewalk they defecate on the neighbor's new flowerbed.

One of my golden retrievers, Aspen, has some Marley genes (I hope you've read John Grogan's book *Marley and Me* or seen the movie). Aspen eats sticky notes off the counter, loves to eat grass, eats the last pages out of novels, and steals and eats washrags, socks, and T-shirts. My wife had a favorite royal-blue shirt that she laid on a chair. Later when she looked for it, she asked me if I'd put it somewhere. I hadn't, but I guessed who did and pointed at the suspect. Tess looked at Aspen. "Aspen, did you take my shirt?" He gave her what I call the DDL—"dumb dog look." You know, the "Huh, me?" attitude. The "You're asking *me* that? How could you even think such a thing? I'm shocked."

I cut in. "Aspen did."

"How do you know that?" Tess asked. "He looks so innocent."

"I know Aspen. Besides, I found the remnants outside on the lawn—at least the parts he didn't eat."

Did Aspen look guilty? Nope. Did he repent? Nope.

Sheffield was my first golden retriever, and my wife and I were very attached to him because he came into our lives eight months after our son, Matthew, died. When I was asked to create a video on personality types to go along with one of my books, I decided to use Sheffield as an example of some of the differences since he was more of an extrovert than an introvert and more of a feeler than a thinker (speaking in Myers–Briggs Type Indicator terms). So during the filming I would have him come up at certain points. And he obediently came, *after* he greeted everyone in the audience, which is what an extrovert does. He responded well to my requests to sit, lie down, stay, give a high-five, answer the phone, pick up trash and put it in the trash can.

Everyone was impressed with Sheffield since he was being so obedient and compliant. Well, up to a point, anyway. When we took a break and most of the audience left, Sheffield and I walked to the back. We had to pass the area where the video crew worked. I didn't notice, but they'd left a plate of donuts on a chair next to the aisle. Sheffield noticed though. The smells and the looks were too much for him to resist. Without missing a step, he grabbed half of them and drooled on the rest. I missed it, but other people laughed and told me about it. So much for my "sinless" dog!

When the cameramen came back, they stopped, looked at the plate, looked around, saw Sheffield, and smiled and said, "Aha! Your old nature overtook your new nature, Sheffield. Come on—confess and repent." I'm pretty sure he did neither. Perhaps he needs to memorize the Scripture verse that helped me so much through high school and college:

> No temptation has overtaken you except what is common to mankind. And God is faithful; he will not let you

be tempted beyond what you can bear. But when you are tempted, he will also provide a way out so that you can endure it (1 Corinthians 10:13).

Dogs aren't perfect, and neither are we. At times, we all violate what we know is right or best. Dogs definitely have problems resisting food. One day I failed to pay attention to this trait. I was in a boat fishing with a friend. I had my sheltie, Prince, along. On my line I had a double set of hooks about a foot apart that were baited with cheese. I turned my head for a second, and when I turned back I saw my line and one of the leaders with bait still dangling but the other hook…well, it was down Prince's throat. We left the lake as fast as we could and rushed him to the vet. Fortunately, he was fine, but it was several agonizing hours before we reached that point. The situation wasn't Prince's fault; it was mine. I put temptation in his way. In spiritual terms, I caused him to stumble.

When we do what we know we shouldn't, we get into difficulty. Temptations are always around us, and sin often appears so attractive…so enticing. We're a bit like dogs. We need training to avoid temptation and stay safe physically and spiritually. Humans have a bent toward doing wrong. In Christian terms, it's called the "old nature." Second Corinthians 5:17 NASB says, "If anyone is in Christ, he is a new creature; the old things passed away; behold, new things have come." Like it says in Romans 3:23: "All have sinned and fall short of the glory of God." The consequences and solution are recorded in Romans 6:23: "The wages of sin is death, but the gift of God is eternal life in Christ Jesus our Lord."

Dogs have instincts; we have the reasoning power to make logical choices. Sometimes we choose well; sometimes we don't. What can help us stay on track? First Corinthians 10:13, which I cited a few paragraphs ago, can make a difference. It did in my life. I memorized it in high school and remember it to this day. Over the years there have been numerous occasions when I've had a choice of doing something right or wrong. The Holy Spirit brought that verse to my mind, and it acted like a guide to keep me on the right track. (I admit that I didn't always appreciate the reminder at the time.)

But what if we do blow it? What about when we sin? God has given us a solution! "If we confess our sins, [God] is faithful and just and will forgive us our sins and purify us from all unrighteousness" (1 John 1:9). God isn't out to punish us when we sin. He wants to restore our relationship with Him that is interrupted by our sin, so He provided a way for that to occur. He is such an awesome God! Why not pause right now and thank Him for His grace and provision?

The Nose Knows

"Stop sniffing there! Stop it, I say. Why do you have to sniff everything and everyone? Yuck. That's disgusting. Be a good dog and stop it." Have you heard dog owners say that? Have you ever said it? My guess is that you have. When we do that, we're asking our dogs to go counter to the way God made them. Dogs were made to sniff and smell *everything*. Most dog owners understand this, but some don't. For some people, a dog's nose action can be a source of embarrassment even though it doesn't seem to be for the dog.

It's true, dogs sniff constantly. They're smelling here, there, and everywhere. They have no boundaries when it comes to sniffing and smelling. It's just what they do, and they're good at it. In fact, their sense of smell is much better than ours. If dogs could praise God, I think He would hear a lot of thank-you barking. Dogs are olfactory gifted. Compared to dogs, you and I are olfactory challenged. A dog's sense of smell is a thousand times more powerful than ours. Dogs discover life through their noses. Dogs would probably say, "I sniff, therefore I am."

Noses come in various sizes and shapes on humans and dogs. Some are long and narrow, others are wide and pug. Some tilt up, while others are plain and simple. I don't know many dogs who would want to have a nose job or alteration like some people do. For most dogs, their noses dominate their face, and their sense of smell dominates their brains and colors their world. Our dogs smell things we'll never smell. Their noses are structured and designed to pick up even the faintest of odors.

A dog also works harder than we usually do to gather scents. We might let scents drift across our noses without paying heed, but they don't. They gather them, sift them, and act on them.

Have you noticed your dog panting? That air goes through their nasal passages and continues on down to the lungs. But when they sniff, that's a different story. That air is stored in the upper chambers of the nose so its contents can be interpreted.

Have you ever been sleeping when all of a sudden you wake up feeling something wet and cold on your face? Surprise! It's your dog's nose. Have you wondered why dog noses are cold and wet? We don't know for sure, but there are a few theories. One is that a dog's nose is wet because the pup constantly licks it. Another is that a dog's nose needs moisture to help the mucous capture scents. The mucous glands capture odor molecules. These are then brought into the nose to special cells that can identify the various smells. It can take a lot of mucous for this to work. Here's a story about the condition of a dog's nose:

> It all began at the time of the great flood, when Noah had collected all of the animals in his ark to save them from the rising water. Since the two dogs on the ark were both clever and reliable, Noah gave them the job of keeping watch for any trouble. One day the dogs were patrolling the ark and noticed that it had sprung a leak. The hole was only about the size of a quarter, but water was pouring in, and if the hole was not repaired, the ark would sink. While one of the dogs quickly ran for help, the other dog did a truly brave and clever thing. He marched up to the leak and stuck his nose into the hole to stop the flow of the water. By the time Noah and his sons arrived to repair the leak, the poor dog was in great pain and gasping for breath. But the dog's brave deed had saved the ark from sinking...[So] God gave the dog his cold, wet nose as a badge of honor and to remind the world of his brave deed.[1]

Dog breeds vary in their ability to identify odor. Those with larger noses have an edge on other breeds. The dachshund has about 125 million smell-receptor cells, and the German shepherd has about 225 million. The bloodhound has around 300 million! Some dogs are trained to find narcotics, explosives, cadavers, arson sources, and even diseases, such as cancer. In one of the novels I was reading I came across a statement that says it all:

Dogs are the cheapest, most reliable bomb detectors in the world. One of my dogs can screen an entire airport in a couple of hours. So they'll burn through this whole park in no time. The dogs find bomb residue my guys won't even be able to see with all our fancy technology...There aren't even any machines in existence that can measure accurately the power of a dog's nose.[2]

Different breeds prefer different methods of following a scent:

Tracking is the most precise means of following an individual, since the dog follows the track...with his nose down, moving from one footstep to the next.

Trailing is the most common way that dogs follow scent paths, by scenting the flakes of scurf [skin cells] shed by the body rather than the footsteps themselves. Because scent rafts drift as they fall, depending upon the wind speed and direction, the dogs may follow directly along the person's path but [they] also may be many yards away, walking parallel to it.

In both tracking and trailing, the dogs can easily find people at night, when human vision is of little value. Tracking and trailing dogs are almost always kept on a long leash while following a scent trail so that they don't outrun their handlers in their enthusiasm to follow the track.

An alternative to tracking and trailing is air-scenting, in which dogs run with their heads up trying to catch the person's scent and ranging around the area until they do. Once the dog catches the scent, he follows it directly to the person, moving in a straight line upwind rather than following the actual path.

Bloodhounds are the best at trailing. They have a great memory for scents.[3]

The records for the ability to follow the oldest scent is held by three bloodhounds: Doc Holliday, Big Nose Kate, and Queen Guinevere. These three were able to pick up a scent that was nearly two weeks old and locate a family of three who had been lost in an Oregon forest. The record for the longest trail ever followed by a dog is currently 135 miles.[4]

Some dogs can catch the scent of a person underwater, underground (cadavers), buried in snow (avalanches), and covered under tons of rubble (earthquakes and terrorist attacks).

Some dogs are used in "scent lineups" to identify perpetrators of crimes. We humans use a visual lineup of people, but not dogs. An item associated with a crime is given to the dog to smell. He's given several other items and then is asked to identify the person associated with the item. Since the dogs are accurate 80 percent of the time, some countries accept this as evidence in court.[5]

Dogs can also sniff out termites and other pests. Home owners know it's almost impossible to locate the little monsters once they've embarked on their obsessive mission to destroy a home. But these pests emit a scent all their own, and a dog's super nose can detect them and pinpoint their headquarters for an exterminator.[6]

There are some dogs that seem to have the ability to detect cancer in humans. Several cases describe dogs detecting and bringing to their owner's attention moles or skin lesions which turn out to be cancerous. Research in this area is growing.

Dogs don't care for some smells, such as citrus or spicy.

Well, this may have been more information than you wanted to know about your dog's nose. I've never met a dog that complained about the size, shape, color, or ability of this gift. They seem to accept and be at peace about their bodies. I wish I could say the same about people. We tend to be so critical of ourselves rather than rejoicing that we are God's creations.

How do you feel about yourself? Are you accepting or critical? Look in the mirror. What do you see? What do you say in your mind about yourself? Is it healthy or unhealthy? Positive or negative? We all talk to ourselves; that's normal. But for most individuals, the majority of their messages to themselves is negative. Do you believe in yourself? God does! He believes in you. And the One who believes in you is the One who asks you to believe in Him.

God doesn't compare you with the other people He's created. He's given you your own unique capabilities and potential. He expects you to develop and use what He's given you, not be envious or want what He's given someone else. He wants you to develop and use what you have so you won't miss out on life. You are God's workmanship!

> We are His workmanship, created in Christ Jesus for good works, which God prepared beforehand so that we would walk in them (Ephesians 2:10 NASB).

Jesus Christ invites us to come to Him by faith, believing that He will accept us as we are into His family:

> As many as received Him, to them He gave the right to become children of God, even to those who believe in His name, who were born, not of blood nor of the will of the flesh nor of the will of man, but of God (John 1:12-13 NASB).

Read these Scriptures too:

> You have made him a little lower than God, and You crown him with glory and majesty! (Psalm 8:5 NASB).

> See how great a love the Father has bestowed on us, that we would be called children of God; and such we are. For this reason the world does not know us, because it did not know Him (1 John 3:1 NASB).

God loves all people, and it grieves Him that people sin and have been separated from Him. He wants to reconcile us to Himself so He sent His Son to us. Even though we are sinful people, we're valuable to God because He loves us. He sees us for the redeemable value we have through Him. That means we ought to love all people too—including ourselves. Dr. Lloyd Ahlem, in *Do I Have to Be Me?*, so clearly summarizes what God has done for us:

> The writers of the Scriptures are careful to point out that when God looks at you in Jesus Christ, He sees you as a brother to His own Son...You are worth all of God's attention. If you were the only person in the world, it would be worth God's effort to make Himself known to you and to love you. He gives you freely the status and adequacy of an heir to the universe.[7]

Do Dogs Have Personality?

Do you have a personality? Of course you do. Does your dog? Definitely. The big question is whether your personalities blend or clash. Is there an acceptance of the uniqueness of each other? People deal with personality issues constantly. For years I provided premarital and marital counseling. Much of the time was spent helping individuals understand their own and their partner's personality traits, learn how to adapt to each other, and, ultimately, come to the place of celebrating their uniqueness and differences.

Since everyone's personality is different, harmony in a family comes not from trying to change the others into an edition of yourself, but in understanding the uniqueness of the others, accepting who they are, and learning to not only adapt your responses to fit them but to also be thankful for who they are.

How can an extrovert and introvert learn to get along? By understanding and accepting each other. For example, an introvert can realize that extroverts think out loud as they sort through options, so what they say doesn't necessarily mean that's what they really believe or will do. Extroverts can offer several compliments through the day and encourage introverts to connect with people. An extrovert can interact with an introvert by saying, "Here's a question I have for you. Why don't you think about it for a while and then let me know what you think." Extroverts can encourage introverts to take some private time to recharge and be aware that being around people a lot makes introverts nervous.

It may not surprise you to know that we tend to pick out dogs that match our personalities. For instance, you may be an extrovert. You're outgoing and enjoy being with people. You get energy from them, need to talk in order to think (you often speak before thinking), have many friends, brainstorm out loud, and have a high need for affirmation. You like being the center of attention. You may not believe you've done a good job until you hear it from others. Now, if that's the case, what type of dog would you prefer?

On the other hand, you may be an introvert. You can be drained by people, prefer one-on-one contact, get energy from being alone, need to think before you speak, and wish others would give you time to say your piece. You tend to be suspicious of compliments. You don't like being the center of attention. What kind of dog do you think you'd prefer?

Are you wondering, "What does personality have to do with dog ownership? Why is understanding personality so important?" It's the reason so many human/dog relationships fall apart (as well as people relationships). The main reason people offer for giving up a dog is its personality or behavior. It's usually not that the dog was bad or the owner insensitive—they were just incompatible. A different matchup would have worked. You see, dogs and humans *are* alike emotionally and share similar personality traits. Personality is different than general characteristics of a particular breed. For example, some terriers are persistent in obtaining their goal, German shepherds tend to be businesslike, and golden retrievers are gregarious.

Why do we like to look at all the puppies in a litter when choosing one instead of having someone pick it out for us? We want to see the personalities of the puppies. Sometimes in human matchups we're drawn to opposites, but that's not a good idea in a human/dog match. Instead, the key factor needs to be *similarity*. One dog trainer, Bonnie Bergin, describes this connection principle:

> The most successful connection between pet and owner occurs with two beings who are so highly matched they become almost one. The key is synchrony, not balance. If

you are trying to reach the stars, you don't want your dog pulling you back to earth. And if you are content to remain on earth, you don't want your dog surging ahead into the outer cosmos.[1]

If a low-key, gentle, introspective person chose a strong-minded, outgoing, energetic male lab, going for walks would be a disaster. But an emotionally sensitive, physically gentle, and quickly responsive dog would be a better match. So the basic principle is similarity. And the relationship works out best when the human is slightly more assertive and slightly more interested in social interaction than the dog.[2] Why is this important? It works. This is the ideal relationship. It's better if your dog instigates nothing *you* don't want and it's ready and willing to go along with everything you start.[3] Remember, dogs look for leadership. You need to be the top dog in the pack. If they don't find it, guess what? They will try to assume the leadership role. That's why dogs often act out more with your children than with you. Your dog knows they're not the leader of the pack so the relationship is different. The leader (you)/follower (your dog) dynamic exists with minimal effort once dominance is established. Take a look at your relationship with your pup now. Are you the leader? Do your personalities blend well?

What About Breed?

Not only can a personality mismatch be a problem, but so can selecting the wrong breed for the purpose you have in owning a dog. Think back for a moment. Why did you want a dog? Some people make a list of the characteristics and qualities they want in a dog. Did you do that?

Let's say you've decided to select a dog. Will you get a male or a female? Will you go for large, small, or medium size? Long hair or short hair? Protective or happy-go-lucky? Outdoor or indoor? You want to establish what type of a relationship you want with your dog.

Are you looking for a watchdog? One that will alert you to the presence of a stranger?

Are you looking for a guard dog? One that will keep people away from your domain?

Are you looking for a child substitute? Some dogs love to be mothered and fathered and enjoy being cuddled.

How about a working partner? This dog would go running, hunting, and sledding with you. Perhaps you'd like to partner with a dog in competition dog trials?

What about a playmate? Are you looking for a physically active dog?

What about a playmate for your children? That would probably be a physically active dog that is also gentle.

Do you want a friend, a companion? Then you'd want a dog with a lot of loyalty.

Some want a show dog that reflects class and beauty.

If you want a dog that has a couple of these qualities, you can probably find one. But no dog can fulfill all of these desires. Once you know what you want, then personality comes into play.

In some ways, choosing a dog is so similar to getting married. Most people have a certain type of person they're looking for. I had a friend who had a list of 14 qualities he was looking for in a wife, and he evaluated each eligible woman he met on a scale of 1 to 10 on each trait. (Yes, it took him years to find someone, and by then the list had been modified.)

Harmony in our relationships can happen, but we will sometimes have to work at it. It's easy to become frustrated and angry in our relationships with family members, friends, and even our pets. Too often people and animals don't respond the way we want or expect, so we want them to change. Can you relate? Perhaps there's a better way:

> [Living as becomes you] with complete lowliness of mind (humility) and meekness (unselfishness, gentleness, mildness), with patience, bearing with one another and making allowances because you love one another (Ephesians 4:2 AMP).

For years I've used this verse when counseling married couples, especially the "living as becomes you" and "making allowance because you love one another" parts. Making allowances for each other means couples can live together with the understanding of who the other person is, accept his or her uniqueness, and adapt responses to suit the other person's bent. And you know what? It works! God is so understanding and accepting of us, and He calls us to be the same with others. This means looking at those around us with a different viewpoint.

And that's not just in relation to people. Your dog probably won't change much, and neither will mine. But as humans, you and I can. And that can make all the difference in whether a relationship will work or not. Perhaps that's something to pray about.

Homing Instinct

Over the years I've read numerous stories of dogs that have been separated from their owners. Perhaps they ran away, or jumped out of a car on a trip, or were stolen. The amazing part of many stories is how the dogs traveled hundreds of miles—or even further—to be reunited with their masters. How did they accomplish such a journey? What led them back to the same location? And how did they manage to locate their owners?

One of the most incredible stories I've heard was of a little terrier named Hector. He actually stowed away on a ship and traveled overseas to another country to find his owner!

A ship's officer was overseeing the loading of cargo on a freighter when he noticed this black-and-white terrier walking up the gangplank. When the dog got on deck, he walked all around and sniffed at different objects. Then he walked back down the gangplank to the shore. Several times that day, Hector went to different ships, looked them over, went up the gangplanks, inspected by sniffing, and then left. He did this on four ships. It wasn't a random checking. He had a purpose, a mission.

The officer who saw Hector didn't give him much thought since he had to get his ship ready for a trip to Yokohama, Japan. A couple of days after setting sail, he noticed Hector walking around the deck. The dog had come aboard and stowed away. He was welcomed by everyone and helped by standing watch each night. Three weeks later, as the ship was unloading some of its cargo, Hector became agitated. He paced back and forth getting more restless as they approached a Dutch ship, the S.S. Simolear. It too was in the process of unloading. Several hours later, some officers and crew members from the Simolear boarded a sampan to ride over to the customs landing. Hector went wild. He jumped up and down and barked as the sampan passed close to the ship. It even looked like he was going to jump overboard!

Finally one of the crew on the sampan heard the barking and looked up. He waved his arms and shouted. Minutes later, the stowaway dog and his master were reunited! Hector's owner told how Hector and he had become separated in Vancouver while the ship was being loaded. Ships are on strict timetables, so there was no time to search for the dog. The ship sailed without Hector. But Hector never gave up. He looked for ways to find his master. What a reunion they had!

How did Hector find the one ship that would take him to where his master was? Was it because of the similarity of the cargo both ships carried? Were there other signs? Did he attach himself to an officer whose duties were similar to his master's? Who knows? Do dogs have some kind of sense we don't know about? There are many unanswered questions when it comes to our canine friends.[1]

Perhaps there's a lesson here for us as well. Sometimes we get into the same situation. We've become separated from God. For some it's a definite break. They've made the choice to live a different lifestyle. Sometimes this occurs following a tragedy. We question God, which is all right, but then we decide not to include Him in our lives and we go our own way. We want reasons for what's happened, and since there isn't one within our understanding, we ask "why?" over and over again. That's what the psalmist did:

Why, LORD, do you stand far off? Why do you hide yourself in times of trouble?" (Psalm 10:1).

How long, LORD? Will you forget me forever? How long will you hide your face from me? (13:1).

Job also questioned God:

Why did I not perish at birth, and die as I came from the womb? (Job 3:11).

Why is light given to those in misery, and life to the bitter of soul...? (3:20).

Jesus questioned His Father too:

Jesus cried out in a loud voice, *"Eloi, Eloi, lema sabachthani?"* (which means "My God, my God, why have you forsaken me?") (Mark 15:34).

Sometimes our disconnect from our Master is subtle and gradual. It could begin by missing a day of praying or reading Scripture one week. The next week we miss a couple of days, and soon a new pattern has developed. The same pattern gradually affects attending church and small group fellowships.

Has this ever happened to you? It has with me. When it does, there's a void in our lives. Something is missing. We have our reasons for our drifting, but that's all they are—human justification for stepping away from God. Years ago there was a popular bumper sticker that read, "If you're not close to God this week, guess who moved?"

If you become disconnected from God, I hope you will search for Him with the same intensity and tenacity of the dogs we've heard stories about. Nothing hindered them. Nothing stopped them. Nothing was able to detour them. They were focused on reuniting with their families.

I wonder what the conversation would be like when someone who drifted from his or her relationship with God reconnected. Perhaps it would sound a lot like this:

Human: Uh, God, it's me.

God: I know.

Human: I've been away…for a while.

God: I know.

Human: But I'm back now.

God: I'm glad.

Human: I've missed You…much more than I realized I would.

God: I've missed you too.

Human: I just want to say I'm sorry I left.

God: I'm glad you returned!

Human: I'd like a close relationship with You again, just like we had before.

God: Hmmm…Let's have a *new* relationship, one that is stronger, deeper, and more committed this time. I would like that much better.

Human: I would too.

God: Welcome back!

Remember the story of Job? He lost his family, his wealth, and his health. At the end of the book of Job, we find out that Job received a new family as well as abundant possessions and his health. Many believe that's what the story of Job is all about. He lost everything, but then he got it all back. But that's not it. The *real* story is how Job found his way home again and established a stronger, more dynamic relationship with God. Job said to God, "My ears had heard of you before, but now my eyes have seen you" (Job 42:5).

Wherever you are today in your relationship with God, I pray you will have a deeper, stronger one with Him tomorrow.

You've Got to Be Kidding!

Some dog owners provide their pets with the basics of life. After all, a dog is just a dog, isn't he? Every now and then we'll find people who appear to be slaves to their dogs. Their lives are dominated by their pooches. They cater to them. This story from *Tails from the Bark Side* by Brian Kilcommons and Sarah Wilson is entertaining and eye-opening:

> Muffin, an older Shepherd mix, arrived at our home with a veritable vanload of survival gear. Along with five meals a day, each in its own labeled plastic container, numerous toys, a special blanket, medical supplies, graham crackers, flashlights, Q-Tips, cotton balls, and more, we got the following set of typed instructions for her care. We offer it to you, we swear, exactly as it was handed to us:
>
> > Muffin is fed five times per day, at 7:00 A.M., 10:30 A.M., 1:30 P.M., 5:30 P.M., and 9:00 P.M. The prepared servings are labeled for the corresponding meals. They should be heated to room temperature to take off the chill. (If she is licking her chops and looks like she is bringing something up in her throat, feed her the 10:30 A.M. feeding early, but no earlier than 10:00 A.M. If this happens, she can be fed the 1:30 meal at 1:15 but no earlier, only if necessary—she will let you know.) Please do not mix up the

times of the labeled meals because some contain vitamins she can only tolerate at certain times of the day.

She should have a generous dollop of chicken soup with meals, heated to room temperature to take off the chill and blended in with the rest of her meal to smooth out the food into a creamy, pudding consistency. Water should be at room temperature, unless it is extremely hot outside, then it can be cool.

She can have a slice of roast beef torn into bite sizes as a snack. It should also be heated to room temperature.

She gets brewer's yeast pills two times per day, at 10:30 A.M. and at 5:30 P.M. She gets three pills each time. Tell her to "chew, chew, chew." (Yes, we do say it three times, otherwise she will swallow it whole.) Give her one pill at a time, not all three at once. She knows brewer's yeast as "b y's."

If she gets sick, it will usually be between 5:00 A.M. and 6:30 A.M. If this happens, she will regurgitate bile, usually between one and three mouthfuls. After this happens, she may look guilty, as if she has done something wrong. We reassure her that she did not. Tell her she is a good girl (lots of positive reinforcement). We give her a tablespoon of Coca-Cola syrup, which normally settles her stomach. This is not an incident that would require veterinary care. Take her outside immediately and let her run it off. If she gets sick more than once in the morning, and is accompanied by diarrhea, phone us immediately. You can usually tell if she is going to get sick. She gets a "look" in her eyes. Her eyes are usually bright, sparkly and clear; if sick, she gets a cloudy cast look in her eyes.

Okay. Now, believe it or not…If you are having a hard time getting her to go out, tell her to go "o u t"—she understands the spelling and will listen.

When you take her out, tell her to "go make doody";

she usually will. She needs to go out first thing in the morning, before she is fed. Do not leave her unsupervised in areas where there is dog stool or grass. She will eat it. Frequent trips outside in the morning (two or three times) will probably alleviate any problems. She will have two bowel movements per day. If she gets runny, mix in ¼ teaspoon only of Tylan powder daily in her food. Let her go out after meals.

If there are thunderstorms, she becomes extremely frightened. Letting her lie down on the bathroom rug we brought will usually calm her down. Tell her to lie down on Magic Carpet. It helps greatly to close any venetian blinds in the room, put on an air conditioner, and turn the volume of the TV or radio up to drown out the thunder. If she could stay with someone it would comfort her.

Important—her nicknames are Muffy, Bubba Angel Bear, Boo Boo Baby Bear, Fin-fin (for Sarah—Mommy's Little Baby), Kabooba Baby Bear, or any combination of the above. Anything with a Baby in it. She likes "Where's Mommy's Little…" preceding it. She likes her tush and hind legs rubbed. If necessary, brush and comb her.

On Sunday, her ears should be cleaned and dried using a cotton swab saturated with Ou-Clens to clean and cotton balls to dry. We put a flashlight in for your use. Then put a dab of ointment in each ear, one at a time, and massage gently. Also, please put her blanket in her cage with her.

On Saturday night and Monday night, if possible, Muffin's teeth need to be brushed. Pleases use both brushes.

Her favorite toy is the pacifier (she knows it as "Binky"). She also knows Booda rope ("Booda"), Tweety Bird, sterilized bones (Kerchunkle bone—because when she drops it, it makes a *kerchunk* noise), Dino bone, Frisbee is her favorite outdoor toy. If someone could play Frisbee with her, she would really enjoy it.

This may seem like a lot of work, but it really isn't. The day goes by very quickly and is usually uneventful. We do not call her a dog—she is a "puppy person." In addition, she is not spoiled, only well maintained.

She is sensitive and needs lots of positive reinforcement and TLC. She likes to be told she is a good girl and is wonderful. She is extremely well behaved and you will find she is very little trouble. She is very affectionate and likes to give lots of kisses, especially on the face. She gets along well with other dogs.

Yes, you must return her to us after the weekend.

As an addendum, during her stay with us, Muffin showed no response to her name, praise, or any of the words in her expansive vocabulary. She slept most of the time, exhibiting zero stress or anxiety, regardless of the noise level. She showed every sign of being a normal, if supremely phlegmatic, dog.[1]

I bet you thought, "You've got to be kidding!" or "Are you serious?" or "Someone needs to go to the vet, and I don't think it's the dog!" or even "Unreal—just unreal." But I'm also sure a smile came to your face or you laughed out loud. I hope you did. We all need to laugh—especially at what's funny or ridiculous. There's enough seriousness in life, and our dogs one way or another can provide us with some laughs.

Scripture has a lot to say about joy and laughter, including these verses:

[There is] a time to weep and a time to laugh, a time to mourn and a time to dance (Ecclesiastes 3:4).

A happy heart makes the face cheerful, but heartache crushes the spirit (Proverbs 15:13).

All the days of the oppressed are wretched, but the cheerful heart has a continual feast (15:15).

A cheerful heart is good medicine, but a crushed spirit dries up the bones (17:22).

How is your sense of humor? Are the times in which we live reflected in your attitude, your face, your outlook? Solomon talks straight, friend. He (under the Holy Spirit's direction) says three things will occur when we have lost our sense of humor: a broken spirit, a lack of inner healing, and dried-up bones. What a barren portrait! I encourage you to look for the positives and trust in the Lord to provide so you can maintain an upbeat outlook.

Humor is not a sin. It is a God-given escape hatch...a safety valve. Being able to see the light of life is a rare, vital virtue.[2]

Change?

Dogs can be creatures of habit, and so can we. Routines are comfortable. Sometimes I think my golden retrievers have built-in clocks. They line up at certain times like they know what's supposed to happen. Every now and then I change things up on them. In the evening is time for a favorite activity. We call it the W-A-L-K. Sorry…I spelled it out. I've learned to do that with certain words, including B-A-L-L and R-I-D-E. If my pups hear those words, they expect the activity to happen immediately. It doesn't work to say, "We'll do it later" because that doesn't register with them. When we go for walks, they know where to stop so I can put on their leashes. Then we head down our long driveway and turn right. They've become wired to do this. If I turn left, they're thrown a tad by the switch. Even if I just switch which dog walks closest to my left leg, it's unfamiliar to them so they're a bit resistant.

I know change is sometimes necessary, but I still resist it too. How about you? It's okay to admit it. We get comfortable with our routines. It's not that we can't change; it's just that we'd rather not. We know not all change is bad, but we don't want to move out of our comfort zone to experience it.

To some, the word "change" holds a sense of hope, connoting fresh possibilities and the potential for newness. They embrace it accordingly. To others, even the very word "change" represents a threat, a disruption of comfort and safety, so they resist. Some make outward or cosmetic changes but intentionally strive to keep the essence of everything statistically the same.

These days we're seeing more changes than most people can handle. Just about the time we get used to a new computer, printer, cell phone, or tablet, it's out of date. By the time we make our first few payments on new cars, newer models are being introduced. Every few months new editions of pet supply catalogs come out. Page after page has the word *New* blazed across them. And we study it. Who knows? There could really be the best dog brush ever made, or the best chew toy, or the best outfit. (Yes, there are dog outfits, but not for my dogs.)

But let's think about another change for a minute. In what ways are you different today than you were five years ago (aside from the obvious, such as age)? Hopefully changes have improved the quality of your character. We all need to change in some ways. It's part of growing.

Although change is part of our lives, God is known by His *changelessness*. Imagine this scenario. You're at work and someone walks into the office and makes this statement:

> Let me tell you something about God that you may not know. God doesn't ever learn a thing. He knows all things. He doesn't have to go around spying on people to discover what's going on. He knows. Remember when you were in school and struggled to learn something? Well, God cannot learn and has never learned. He doesn't need to. He knows everything instantly. He knows everything equally well. He never wonders about anything, never discovers anything, and is never amazed by anything. He also knows all the possibilities that can happen.[1]

God doesn't change. Created things have a beginning and ending, but God doesn't. He has always been and always will be. There was not a time when He didn't exist. He doesn't grow older. He doesn't get wiser. He doesn't grow stronger or weaker. He can't change for the better because He's already perfection. Scripture confirms this:

They shall perish, but you go on forever. They will grow old
like worn-out clothing, and you will change them like a man
putting on a new shirt and throwing away the old one! But
you yourself never grow old. You are forever, and your years
never end (Psalm 102:26-27 TLB).

God's character doesn't change either. He *is* truth. His truth does
not change. Because He is mercy, He never has to take back what He's
said or done. His mercies toward us are new every morning. Because
He *is* goodness, we can know that every good and perfect gift comes
from Him. Because Jesus is the promised Lamb of God, we can trust
in His promises and know that He will fulfill them concerning our
lives. God's purposes don't change. What He does in the context of
time, He planned from eternity. All that He has committed Himself
to do in His Word will be done.

James speaks about God as One "with whom there is no variation
or shadow due to change" (James 1:17 RSV). This refers to the fact that
when a sundial is at high noon, it doesn't cast a shadow. God is always
at high noon for us. We can depend on Him. What a comfort! It's
difficult for us to understand everything about God. But our inability to comprehend gives evidence to the vast difference between God
and the people He created.[2] Discovering that we can count on God
not changing gives us stability.

So, if you or your dogs resist change, that's normal. But change can
be good for us because it's evidence that we can grow.

Frank

Let me tell you about a friend. He's big. He's like a gentle giant. Most of the time he's quiet—he doesn't say much. He doesn't usually have to because his presence is so commanding. I see him once in a while because we're both engaged in the same type of work.

I'm a grief and trauma therapist; so is Frank.

Recently I've been helping at a high school in Taft, California. So has Frank. One winter day in 2013, a student came to that school with a shotgun, went into his first-period class, took aim, and shot a fellow student. He shot one more time but fortunately missed everyone else. At that point the teacher talked him into putting the gun down. By then the damage was done. The young man who was shot survived, but he will carry the physical wounds the rest of his life. All 28 students and the teacher were traumatized and will carry the emotional wounds for years, and some maybe for life.

The entire school, staff, and students were affected by this event. This was a terrible occurrence, and our team of counselors and responders had been working there for months. Some students were experiencing flashbacks, anxiety, hyper-vigilance, intrusive thoughts, discomfort with being alone, difficulty sleeping, concentration issues, anxiety, anger, rage. These are all of the symptoms of Post Traumatic Stress Disorder (PTSD).

I arrived to help three days after the incident. So did Frank.

I sit with individual students as well as small groups to help people recover. So does Frank.

But there are also differences between Frank and me. I'm *a lot* older than the students. Frank is closer to their age.

I listen but I also talk and share and suggest. Frank just listens.

When I walk into the school and out onto the quad where students are gathered, they really don't notice me that much. They notice Frank right away. When he appears it's as though time comes to a halt. Conversations die down and stop. Heads turn toward him. A few leave their groups and walk toward him. He turns toward them and smiles. Hands reach out to touch him. He responds gently and quietly.

Frank is large and stately. Most Newfoundland's are. Frank has a mission. He's a therapy dog. He goes to the school once or twice a week, but not to show off. With his beautiful black-and-white markings he certainly could. He has a regal look. He provides a sense of calm to the traumatized high school kids. They talk to him and stroke his fur, and their upset and grief diminishes. For a time their hypervigilance and fear subside. A few moments with Frank makes their lives better and restores the sense of school being a safe haven again. Frank has other coworkers with him—a sheepdog, a lab, a French bulldog. They too are helping the students.

After a couple of hours, Frank and his friends leave. They've done their job. They need to leave since the stress, anxiety, and grief of the students has been transferred to them, and they too can handle just so much.

Like those students, we have the trauma and upsets that occur in our lives as well. We need someone who has a calming presence that we can share and transfer our stress and anxiety with. And we do! And our Comforter, unlike the rest of us, can handle all of what we need to unload. He never tires and is never overwhelmed by what we need. He has a calming effect that goes well beyond what Frank, his friends, and counselors can provide.

I'm thankful for Frank. I've known him for a few years now. But I'm more thankful for the One I've known most of my life—our heavenly Father. Read the following Scriptures out loud each morning and evening for the next month. You will be amazed at the results!

> You will keep in perfect peace those whose minds are steadfast, because they trust in you (Isaiah 26:3).

> When my anxious thoughts multiply within me, Your consolations delight my soul (Psalm 94:19 NASB).

> So do not fear, for I am with you; do not be dismayed, for I am your God. I will strengthen you and help you; I will uphold you with my righteous right hand (Isaiah 41:10).

> God is our refuge and strength, an ever-present help in trouble. Therefore we will not fear, though the earth give way and the mountains fall into the heart of the sea, though its waters roar and foam and the mountains quake with their surging. There is a river whose streams make glad the city of God, the holy place where the Most High dwells. God is within her, she will not fall; God will help her at break of day (Psalm 46:1-5).

Lost and Rescued

I was driving down the street and my eye caught a sign that I'd seen several times: "Lost Dog!" When I read the print, it gave a description of the dog along with "Reward $500." The people wanted their dog rescued, and the amount of money indicated how valuable this dog was to them. Have you ever lost your dog? For some it's just a few minutes, and others it's for days or weeks. It's a sick feeling when our dogs are missing. We tend to pull out all the stops to make sure he or she is rescued. I know, I've been there.

Growing up my dog was a friendly collie named Laddie. Since we lived in the Hollywood Hills in Southern California, we didn't have fenced yards. When Laddie was outside, he needed to be tethered. One day I went out and, to my surprise, he'd chewed through his tether. Laddie was gone!

My parents and I searched. We went up and down the various streets. We called neighbors and told them to be on the lookout for Laddie. Since he was a stay-at-home dog, his disappearance was unusual. We looked for most of the day but no Laddie was found. We didn't sleep very well that night. The next day I went to school, but my mind wasn't really there.

As soon as I got home, we got into the car and expanded our search. We drove on a road that went to the top of a mountain range that had a view overlooking Los Angeles and the ocean. On a clear day we could see 20 miles. We got out and called for Laddie. A few seconds later we heard a faint bark. We heard it again and looked over the steep side of the mountain—and I mean steep!

We soon realized Laddie wasn't coming closer, so we needed to go where the bark was coming from. We slid down the mountain, carefully holding on to brush and avoiding the large cactus plants. When we were about fifty feet down from the top, we found Laddie. He'd caught his collar in a piece of brush and was stuck. He could hardly move! Had we not found him, he would have died in a few days. He was thirsty and hungry but so overjoyed at seeing us and being rescued.

"Rescue" is a word often associated with dogs. There are rescue organizations that focus on most breeds of dogs. Owners sometimes need to find a new home for their dogs because of a change of family status, or a move, or an inability to care for their animals. Instead of taking their dog to the Humane Society or the dog pound, the owners take their dog to a rescue organization where it is cared for until someone wanting this breed comes looking.

We all know of rescue dogs that are used to find people who are lost for one reason or another. Dogs provide rescue in many other ways too. They rescue those with disabilities from a life of confinement by opening up new opportunities and broader horizons. They provide life-changing services to disabled men and women as well as boys and girls. There are numerous programs to provide dogs for those who are visually impaired as well as those who are hearing impaired.

Canine Companions for Independence is such an organization. This group has provided hundreds of trained service dogs to those in need. To those who are physically challenged due to an accident or illness and those who have mental impairments, these dogs have indeed rescued individuals from lives that were confining.[1] Many dogs are trained as service animals for people with disabilities. A service animal is trained to assist a person in one or more activities of daily living. This can include guiding them, giving alerts at sounds, seizure alerts, and emotional support work. Their work is handler-focused. Most places allow service animals to accompany their handlers wherever they go, including concert venues, grocery stores, and restaurants. Service animals are not considered pets and are usually on duty when out with their masters. Their focus is on their masters. The dogs (and occasionally other animals) assist their owners in many ways.

People don't have to have disabilities to need rescued. In fact, every person needs rescued. We're all born with a condition called "sin." We don't have a relationship with God, and our thoughts and behavior don't naturally follow what He wants for us:

> All have sinned and fall short of the glory of God (Romans 3:23).

> The wages of sin is death, but the gift of God is eternal life in Christ Jesus our Lord (6:23).

If anyone needs to be rescued, it's us! Fortunately, God provided a massive rescue operation! It's still in existence and is always available:

> It is by grace you have been saved, through faith—and this is not from yourselves, it is the gift of God—not by works, so that no one can boast (Ephesians 2:8-9).

> God so loved the world that he gave his one and only Son, that whoever believes in him shall not perish but have eternal life (John 3:16).

I pray that you have taken advantage of His great rescue offer!

Peace Is Possible!

Some dogs don't seem to have a care in the world. Even when chaos and confusion reign all around, some dogs don't even look up, wag their tails, or even yawn. You might be upset, but your dog isn't. Perhaps you even wonder if your pup has a pulse!

There are other dogs that remind me of some people I know. They seem to have a "frantic gene." Their bodies move and twitch constantly. It's like they're always in panic mode.

In today's world, many people are like that when it comes to electronics. They're addicted to their devices. Talk about frantic! Have you ever left your cell phone at home or lost track of it for a few hours? You miss the texting sound and the special ring tone that marks a call coming in. Your life—and everything else—stops while you tear the house, car, and office apart until you find it. You feel naked without it, so you look under every pillow, every chair, every possible hiding place. Your eyes scan the room, and you glance at your dog. Your gaze moves on…until it hits you. Herman! Could he have eaten it? He is a 140-pound Great Dane, after all.

"Herman? No, you couldn't have…but…Herman, did you eat my phone? My special phone that has all my information, addresses, and photos? That has all my apps set to just how I want them? How could you!"

What kind of answer do you expect from a dog? Herman looks at you, seems to laugh as his tongue hangs out, stretches, and rolls over, putting all four feet in the air as he looks cute. Did he or didn't he eat the phone? He could have, but he'll never tell. You're frantic and stressed out, but he's cool, calm, and collected. You sit down in frustration. Then you feel it. A little bump on your behind. The phone had slipped out of its case and into your back pocket. Was all that stress worth it?

One morning I met my fishing buddy at a lake. I wish I'd gotten there 10 minutes earlier because I missed what happened. When I arrived he told me about it. It had rained the day before, so the bank was very slick. He had his new cell phone, along with his fishing gear. His first step onto the slope that led to the edge of the water was the only one he had to take. He kept going, and going, and going until he was launched right into four feet of water. Funny thing about electronics. They don't work very well when or after they've been submerged. Needless to say, he wasn't happy about the situation.

Even when we're out of touch, life goes on. The world continues regardless of what we're doing. Perhaps we think we're indispensable, but we're really not. Some people say, "I've got to stay in touch because they might need me." Or, "Hey, it's a cutthroat world out there. You've got to be on your guard. It's not that safe, so I'll stay in touch to help you if you need it." We think we're in control; we think we're in charge of everything. We can't relax. We worry and miss the joy and peace God offers us.

I encourage you to turn your technology off every once in a while to really experience the presence of God. Whether you're at home, at work, or walking the dog, let yourself enter into the presence of Jesus without the possibility of electronic interruptions. Some of the most peaceful and creative times I experience occur when I'm walking my dogs (unless they see a cat!). It's a time I can put my mind on hold and not think about anything. (It's true, men *can* do this. We have "Nothing" lobes in our brains.)

In the Gospel of Matthew, we read that Jesus and His disciples were in a boat when "suddenly, a fierce storm struck the lake, with waves breaking into the boat" (8:24). This was a common occurrence on the Sea of Galilee. The disciples were frantic, but Jesus was peacefully sleeping through it. Here is what one of my favorite authors, John Ortberg, said about this story and what you and I can experience:

> Given what he knew about the Father, Jesus was convinced that the universe was a perfectly safe place for him to be.
>
> The disciples had faith in Jesus. They trusted that he could do something to help them. They did not share his settled conviction that they were safe in God's hands.
>
> This is what Paul called "the peace of Christ."[1]

Perhaps we need to consider what our lives would look like if we lived in the conviction of who God is and in the power of His presence. John described the possible results:

- My anxiety level would go down. I would have the settled trust that my life is perfectly at rest in the hands of God. I would not be tormented by my own inadequacy.

- I would be an unhurried person. I might be busy, might have many things to do, but I would have an inner calmness and poise that comes from being in the presence of God. I would not say so many of the foolish things I now say because I speak without thinking.

- I would not be defeated by guilt. I would live in the confidence that comes from the assurance of God's love.

- I would trust God enough to risk obeying him. I wouldn't have to hoard. Worry makes me focus on myself. It robs me of joy, energy and compassion.

- A person in whom the peace of Christ reigns would be an oasis of sanity in a world of pandemonium.

- A community in which the peace of Christ reigns would change the world.[2]

Up to No Good

A litter of puppies is a delightful sight. The young critters wrestle, chew, bite, pull, and climb all over one another. We laugh at their antics and love to watch them. Do you have that picture in mind? Now, take the same litter of puppies and imagine them as adults. You see this same group of dogs roaming through your neighborhood. What is your response now?

"Oh oh! What are those dogs up to?"

"I'd better keep an eye on them."

"I wonder who owns them and why they're loose."

Your response went from delight to apprehension. The litter has evolved into a pack.

A group of dogs is similar to a group of kids. Let them roam around together, and they might do what they wouldn't do on their own. It's like they've become a mob. Verilese Graeme describes this scenario well: "Mob mentality. In sociology, this is a group of persons stimulating one another to excitement and losing ordinary rational control over their activity." In an article titled "Bears and Dogs in Alaska," Beth Fowler mentions this dog mob tendency: "Most dogs are intimidated by bears, but in the presence of other dogs their pack mentality kicks in and they may give chase. Chasing a bear is not a good thing." I found an enjoyable story in the book *Best Friends Forever—Me and My Dog* by Rebecca Currington I think you'll enjoy. It describes what dogs can do when they run together.

Dogs just like to have fun, and Sage and Clemie are proof positive of that. These yellow American Labrador retrievers are sisters born from the same mother a year apart. Robert, their owner, says Sage, the older of the two, was feisty as a pup. She once chewed up his tennis shoe and unsuccessfully attempted to dig out under the back fence. But overall, she was a good dog. It was normal for her to fetch a stick or two or wrestle around on the ground, maybe even dig up a bone and place it at Robert's feet. If anything, though, she may have been a little too docile.

That's why Robert thought she might need a companion. He was thrilled to hear that Sage's mother had just had a litter of pups. One of the females was still available, and the breeder promised to call as soon as she was weaned. Sage wasn't sure what to do with her at first, but she quickly took a liking to her little sister. Robert named her Clementine (Clemie for short). The adorable little puppy gave Sage a new lease on life.

Then one day Robert got a call at work from a neighbor, who reported seeing Sage and Clemie roughhousing on someone else's front lawn. When he pulled into the driveway, his two recalcitrant pets met him at the car. They stood with guilty faces as he examined the pile of dirt and the hole under the fence. Robert shored up the hole and placed some boards over the soft ground. But a few days later, their remorse forgotten, they escaped again by way of a hole under the front gate.

The first time the dogs made their way to freedom, they seemed surprised to have actually pulled off a successful escape. But this time their boldness must have been intoxicating. There are no human witnesses to what happened after that, except that a woman who lives a few houses down said she saw them running back and forth through the neighborhood earlier in the day. The physical evidence, however, did a good job of documenting the dogs' crime spree. One neighbor's trash can was tipped over and the trash tracked around the side yard; and the man across the street reported several potted plants were toppled over and doggy paw prints could be seen in the newly planted flowerbed. The worst of it, though, took place two houses down on the left.

After several rainy, overcast days, the sun was actually shining, so neighbor Charlotte had decided to sit at her picnic table and fold laundry. "I just went inside for a minute," she later reported to Robert, "just long enough to answer the phone and put another load in the washer." When she came back out, she saw Sage and Clemie and an unidentified perpetrator, described by Charlotte only as "big and brown," playing tug-of-war with one of her good bath towels. The rest of the laundry was strewn about the yard. Her coffee cup was lying in the grass, and all that was left of her partially eaten bran muffin was a torn paper baking cup.

Robert would say that Sage and Clemie aren't really bad dogs. In fact, most of the time they are model citizens. He thinks of them more as two honor students who decided to skip school on senior day and got caught up in some unfortunate incidents. A little sunshine, a random act of rebellion, and bad company can add up to disaster.

It's easy for humans to get into trouble in much the same way. We are sometimes willing to do things in a group that we would never do alone. Things like gossip, racial slurs, intimidation, for example. Let's take a lesson from Sage and Clemie's disastrous day and take care not to be caught up in pack mentality.[1]

How easily we're influenced by others. People too can fall into a crowd mentality. As followers of Jesus, however, we've been called *to influence*, not to be influenced:

Don't copy the behavior and customs of this world, but let God transform you into a new person by changing the way you think (Romans 12:2).

There's trouble ahead when you live only for the approval of others...Your task is to be true, not popular (Luke 6:26 MSG).

How Close Are You?

Some dogs are aloof and distant, while others can't seem to get enough of us. They're what I call "leaners." Wherever you are, they've got to be there *and* be as close to you as possible. Some even have to touch you in some way. We all do, as reflected in this story:

Dogs vary drastically by breed. A St. Bernard and a Chihuahua, for example, would seem to have very little in common. One characteristic, however, is shared by almost every breed, regardless of size, age, color, or temperament: devotion to their masters, despite the fact that in most cases dogs have no say in who that might be. Unlike our dog friends, we have the privilege of choosing whom we will serve. If we choose God, we should demonstrate our devotion even more enthusiastically.

At first take, Holly would seem an unlikely name for a Siberian husky. Of course, seeing the little black-and-white ball of fur playing with the discarded bows from the Christmas morning revelry might add a touch of understanding. A few hours earlier, she had been wearing one of those bows. She was the best Christmas gift Daniel had ever received, or so he kept announcing repeatedly to absolutely anyone who would listen.

Finally, nine-year-old Daniel curled up on the sofa and fell asleep. He'd been awake half the night hoping for a puppy and awake since five trying to persuade his parents to let him check under the tree. Of course, when they finally relented around seven-thirty, he flew down the stairs to find plenty of beautifully wrapped packages, but no puppy. Disappointment was written all over his face. But he quickly turned jubilant when his parents brought the little guy in from the garage a couple of hours later. Boy and dog romped around the living room, and then the garage once the noise level became too much for Daniel's mom. They ended up in the snow-covered front yard where, except for her black nose, perky black-and-white ears, and red bow, Holly would have disappeared all together. By noon it was clear Daniel was no match for her boundless energy.

That was how it all began. Eleven years have passed since that Christmas morning. My nephew Daniel is away at the University of Michigan working on a degree in mechanical engineering. In the meantime, Holly has become his parents' dog. The little puppy is now a full sixty pounds. Peg is fond of telling visitors, "We like to think of Holly as not a dog but more of a smallish cow." And if you saw her from a distance, you might agree, since her ample girth is covered by her fluffy white coat with large black spots.

Holly is still amazingly playful for her age and size. But now in her golden years, her favorite thing to do is to lie on the floor next to Peg or Daniel's father, Roland. Actually, it would be more accurate to say she lies down on them. She just can't seem to get close enough, so she positions herself right on top of their feet and then drops off into a comfortable slumber. When Daniel comes home for the weekend, Holly runs around in a circle—her traditional "happy" dance—but as soon as he puts his stuff away and settles down on the sofa, she lies down on top of his sneakers and nods off.

Holly greets all the Martins' guests enthusiastically. She is gentle and friendly and likes to make strangers, young and old alike, feel welcome. She enjoys being in the room when people are talking and laughing and having fun. She's a big sweetheart of a dog. But lying down at their feet? Well, that's reserved for the very special people in her life, those she is uncompromisingly devoted to. Only with Daniel, Peg and Roland does she demonstrate that she adores them so much she simply can't get close enough. And it's obvious that they adore her as well. Holly's naps tend to run long these days, but they wouldn't think of disturbing her. So they sit with their feet pinned to the floor until the old husky wakes up and sets them free.

When it comes to God, how devoted are we? Do we love being in his presence? Some people go to church in order to feel close to God. But those of us who are most devoted to him are like Holly: We can't get close enough. We aren't satisfied with an arm's-length relationship. We want to move in close and closer until we are at his feet, touching him, feeling his warmth, gathering life, strength and spiritual energy. The Bible assures us that God invites this level of closeness from those who have true, faithful and devoted hearts.[1]

How would you describe a time when you really experienced the closeness of God? When do you feel the closeness of God the most? What could you do today to draw even closer to Him?

Humble yourselves before God. Resist the devil, and he will flee from you. Come close to God, and God will come close to you (James 4:7-8).

You're all I want in heaven! You're all I want on earth! When my skin sags and my bones get brittle, GOD is rock-firm and faithful (Psalm 73:25-26 MSG).

Here's a great quote from a hymn written by Sarah F. Adams:

> Nearer, my God, to Thee, nearer to Thee!
> E'en though it be a cross that raiseth me,
> Still all my song shall be, nearer my God, to Thee!

Saved

My favorite author as a child was Albert Payson Terhune. Mostly he wrote about dogs. Some of his books include *Lochinvar Luck; Lad of Sunnybank; Further Adventures of Lad; Gray Dawn; Buff, A Collie and Other Dog Stories;* and *Treve*. From some of the titles, you can probably guess he primarily wrote about collies. And he wrote with such detail that I felt like I became part of the story and lived it with the people and dogs. I thought about collies and dreamed about them. I asked for a collie for years, and one day when I was recovering from a slight case of polio (this took several months), we went to a kennel and selected a collie. He wasn't a show dog, and he wasn't the prettiest collie, but he was a pup and he was mine. Of course I named him Laddie. He became my friend and constant companion. Every day after school I would take him and my BB gun, and we would roam the hills of Hollywood searching for wild game or cowboys on the run. There weren't other children around where I lived, so Laddie filled a need in my life.

Like most dogs, Laddie loved food—especially people food, including cake. My mom made this great sunshine cake. It was a yellow cake with chocolate frosting. One day when I came home from school she said she'd made the cake. I remember being so excited I could almost taste it in anticipation. Usually cakes were on the counter and protected. But this time, for some reason, Mom put the cake in a lower cupboard in the breakfast room. When I opened the cupboard door, instead of a cake covered in dark frosting there were a few yellow crumbs and some splotches of chocolate. In my shock, it took a few seconds to realize who had eaten it. And he was nowhere around. Laddie either knew he shouldn't have eaten the cake, that he was in deep trouble, that he was feeling guilty, or that he had a stomachache—or hopefully all of these. He recovered from the experience, and Mom never ever put *my* cake anywhere within Laddie's reach again.

Even so, Laddie was very much loved, and he was much more than just a companion. He saved our lives. It's true! I wouldn't be here today were it not for my dog. Laddie slept in what we called our "washing room," located at the back of the house. He was comfortable there, and because the room was adjacent to the kitchen he could enjoy all the smells that sifted under the door.

One night, around two o'clock, a new odor drifted under the door. This was something Laddie hadn't smelled before. As you know, dogs have twenty times the olfactory neurons in their brains than humans do. That means they can smell odors we never know about. Laddie realized that something was amiss. He began to bark and bark. Then his tone grew more urgent. I was the first one to hear him, and I woke Mom up. By then the smoke was intense, and our eyes stung. We realized we had a major problem, and I could hear Laddie barking and scratching at the door. We remembered not to stand, so we got down on the floor and crawled to the outside door. We all got out without injury and went around and freed Laddie. We felt the results of the smoke in our eyes and lungs for a long time, and our clothes reeked of smoke for weeks.

The firemen who came quickly took care of the problem. I'll never forget what one man said: "You can be thankful and grateful to Laddie. If it weren't for him, you wouldn't be here. He saved your life." Our old refrigerator motor had finally worn out, and a hot wire broke and began to smolder against the asbestos. There was no flame, but the smoke increased and drifted through the kitchen and under the door to the washroom before filling the whole house.

Not everyone has an experience like this with his dog, but everyone has had this experience with God. The Scriptures are filled with true stories of God pursuing mankind in order to save us. My life was saved by God's reaching out to me with His gift of salvation through His Son, Jesus. Your life has been saved the same way. Our lives were saved because we heard a warning—a barking, if you will. When we woke up, we didn't debate the warning or go back to sleep. We responded to what it was calling us to do—get up and get out of our lives of sin and rest in the comfort and safety of God's love. God extends His offer of eternal life to all of us. Look at just some of the Scriptures that speak to us about salvation:

I [Jesus] am the gate. Those who come in through me will be saved. They will come and go freely and will find good pastures (John 10:9).

We believe that we are all saved the same way, by the undeserved grace of the Lord Jesus (Acts 15:11).

For if, while we were God's enemies, we were reconciled to him through the death of his Son, how much more, having been reconciled, shall we be saved through his life! (Romans 5:10).

If you declare with your mouth, "Jesus is Lord," and believe in your heart that God raised him from the dead, you will be saved (10:9).

"[God] made us alive with Christ even when we were dead in transgressions—it is by grace you have been saved...For it is by grace you have been saved, through faith—and this is not from yourselves, it is the gift of God" (Ephesians 2:5,8).

Can you remember when you first experienced God's saving grace? Where were you? How old were you? What happened? How has your life been impacted because of this event? It sometimes helps to revisit the beginnings of our walk with God to remember that at one time we *didn't* have eternal life and now we do.

If you're like me, you share stories of your dog with others—the cute, funny, and odd experiences. We all enjoy this. But when was the last time you shared the story of your salvation and the joy of God's presence in your life? It's more important than sharing our dog stories.

That Still Small Voice

Sometimes dogs amaze us. There are many stories of how dogs have saved the day and some have even saved lives. I enjoyed reading stories of what I call "hero dogs." There are so many of these stories that you've probably read some too. We all enjoy hearing about dogs protecting or rescuing people and other animals.

Fritz was a search dog who lived in a valley near the Matterhorn in the Swiss Alps. This area was known for massive snowstorms and blizzards. These are weather events that often bring tragedy to those who are unprepared or careless. Most of the mountain people prepare well, but sometimes they can run short of supplies.

Five of the men in the valley decided to go after firewood since the storm had been so massive. While they were on a slope, a large portion of the snowpack let loose, gathered momentum, and became a treacherous avalanche that overtook them and buried them under tons of snow.

Seventeen men and one dog, Fritz, were sent out to search for the wood gatherers. Fortunately, they found four of them right away and dug them out. They were half frozen but alive. But Fritz wasn't content. He continued to search and sniff, sniff, and sniff. The leader of the rescue group asked the four if there were any others in the group that could have been buried. "Yes, there's one more. Can you find him?" Fritz didn't need anyone to tell him that there was another man. He knew. He could smell. He searched and then stopped to dig through the snow and rocks. The rescue team helped and soon they found the fifth man still alive. And that's the happy conclusion to the story of Fritz's rescue. Or is it?

Fritz was still agitated. He paced and sniffed, but this time he didn't sniff the ground. He kept his nose up and sniffed the air. The rescue workers wondered if there was another survivor, but everyone was accounted for. Fritz started to growl, showed his teeth, and snapped at the rescue leader's legs. He finally got hold of his snowsuit and began to tug and pull and growl. The leader tried to understand Fritz's strange behavior. He finally said, "Something's going on that he senses, and I think he wants us to move." They packed up the stretchers and evacuated the area. A few minutes later, a massive avalanche, larger than the first, covered the area they'd just left. No one would have survived, nor would they have been found.[1]

How did Fritz know what was about to happen? I'm not sure. Regardless of the reason, the dog knew, and lives were saved because of his actions and by the rescue workers heeding his warning.

You and I get prompts all the time. Sometimes we call this intuition. Women experience this much more than men. Sometimes they say, "I just felt it" or "I just knew." We men tend to just shake our heads and question their input; even some women discount their intuition. But why not pay attention and see what happens?

There is another prompting we need to listen to also. Have you felt the Holy Spirit moving in your life? Sometimes we wonder where a thought or a sense or a decision is coming from because it's so different. People will say, "You know, as I was praying I felt led to…" and they followed that leading. Something alerted Fritz to sound a warning. God speaks to us and alerts us through the leading of the Holy Spirit. Some believe this happens regularly, while some think it's rare. I sometimes wonder where some of my ideas and examples for ministry and writing come from.

Years ago when I was in college, I attended Hollywood Presbyterian Church. One morning in the college-age group, the speaker taught on the ministry of the Holy Spirit. He challenged us to go home, bow down in prayer, and ask God for the leading of the Holy Spirit in our lives. I remember doing just that. My parents were gone that weekend, so I had the house to myself. It was a significant time, but not that dramatic. I characterize it as brief rather than extensive. But I realized later that it was life changing. Later that summer I was at the Forest Home College Briefing Conference with several hundred people in attendance. During that week I felt the prompting of the Holy Spirit to go into full-time ministry. That was more than 50 years ago, and I'm still doing it.

Heeding the promptings of the Holy Spirit in our lives is essential. "Walk by the Spirit, and you will not gratify the desires of the flesh" (Galatians 5:16). The ability and power to overcome sin is not by our own power but by the Holy Spirit alive within us. Any spiritual power you and I have comes from the Holy Spirit:

> What we have received is not the spirit of the world, but the Spirit who is from God, so that we may understand what God has freely given us. This is what we speak, not in words taught us by human wisdom but in words taught by the Spirit, explaining spiritual realities with Spirit-taught words. The person without the Spirit does not accept the things that come from the Spirit of God but considers them foolishness, and cannot understand them because they are discerned only through the Spirit (1 Corinthians 2:12-14).

God...

- leads us if we're open

- speaks to us if we listen

- directs us if we submit

- stays active in our lives if we let Him

The Wandering Dog

Come back here! Don't you dare run away!" Are these familiar words? They certainly indicate frustration. A dog is a dog no matter how well behaved he seems to be at the moment or how much training he's had. There's a little gene in most dogs (if not all) that says, "I deserve to get out and run around whenever and wherever I want to go." And no matter what we say or how loud we raise our voices, which often sounds like barking to our dogs and excites them even more, or what treats we promise to give, we're ignored. "How dare that dog ignore me! Look at the easy life he leads here!" we mutter.

But what must the dogs be thinking? Perhaps, "Boy, look at all this room to run around in. And all the smells! Wow! There are other dogs around. I wonder where there are? Ah yes, I smell Rex, and Rascal, and Daisy, and Fred. Who names a dog Fred? Fifi—now there's a dog I'd like to spend some time with. I think I'll go around the block. There are always some cats to chase over there, and their owners leave the cat food out on the porch. Some of those cats need to go a bit hungry. They're downright fat and lazy. I'll just help them out by having a feast. Hey, there's a building with lots of kids playing outside. Oh boy! Kids love me. They let me play ball and share their lunches with me. I just love those Oreo cookies!"

How can we compete with all those distractions? We can scold our dogs, admonish them, praise them, but when they get the desire to take off and explore, it's like they have a radar lock on something other than staying home.

I send one of my goldens out to the driveway to fetch the paper every day. He usually runs out about 200 feet, picks the paper up, turns, and runs back to me. But if he sees another dog in our area while on his mission, he's off. Forget his "Canine Good Citizen Certificate." He's just failed the test. For some dogs, there are always stronger pulls that override their training.

None of us like to have our voices tuned out, but it happens. The author of *Best Friends Forever* wrote:

> Even the best-behaved dog has been know to head out in search of an adventure—the smell of fresh clover, new people to meet and warm breeze replete with the promise of bones yet uncovered. When this happens, the only call that pooch is going to hear is the call of the wild. People also have such lapses. It's possible to become so caught up in our busy lives that we wander off and close our ears to the voice of God.[1]

Scripture also talks about people wandering:

> The LORD's anger burned against Israel and he made them wander in the wilderness forty years, until the whole generation of those who had done evil in his sight was gone (Numbers 32:13).

> [The LORD,] who pours contempt on nobles made them wander in a trackless waste (Psalm 107:40).

> With my whole heart have I sought You, inquiring for and of You and yearning for You; Oh, let me not wander or step aside [either in ignorance or willfully] from Your commandments (Psalm 119:10 AMP, brackets in original).

> [Lord,] You rebuke the proud and arrogant, the accursed ones, who err and wander from Your commandments (Psalm 119:21 AMP).

[Lord,] You spurn and set at nought all those who stray from Your statutes, for their own lying deceives them and their tricks are in vain (Psalm 119:118 AMP).

Such to you shall they [the astrologers and their kind] be, those with whom you have labored and such their fate, those who have done business with you from your youth; they will wander, every one to his own quarter and in his own direction. No one will save you (Isaiah 47:15 AMP, brackets in original).

I remember my affliction and my wandering, the bitterness and the gall (Lamentations 3:19).

How might you and I wander today? Here are some thoughts I shared in my book *A Better Way to Think*:

Our thoughts also wander. Sometimes there's more energy involved in wandering. It can be more active than drifting. We say of a child, "he wandered away" or remark that a husband "wandered from the marriage."

We all have wandering minds. Even when you're focused on a particular subject or speaker or engaged in a personal activity, your mind may wander away from your intended purpose. It's easy to begin daydreaming, planning, fantasizing, or just aimlessly drifting about.

Wandering and getting absorbed in other things is what our minds do. But sometimes our minds wander into areas that feed our problems rather than help resolve them. For example, if you're having problems in your marriage, allowing yourself to think about an attractive person at work isn't a helpful use of your thoughts.

Sometimes we can become entangled where we've allowed ourselves to drift: to future events, past painful encounters, worries and so on.

God understands. Consider this Scripture:

> And you, Solomon my son, know the God of your father
> [have personal knowledge of Him, be acquainted with,
> and understand Him; appreciate, heed and cherish Him]
> and serve Him with a blameless heart and a willing mind.
> For the Lord searches all hearts and minds and under-
> stands all the wanderings of the thoughts. If you seek Him
> [inquiring for and of Him and requiring Him as your first
> and vital necessity] you will find Him; but if you forsake
> Him, He will cast you off forever! (1 Chronicles 28:9 AMP,
> brackets in original).

I might not be aware of all my thoughts, but God certainly is. He "understands all the wanderings of the thoughts."

When I'm listening to the Sunday sermon or to someone who's telling a novel-length story, my mind wanders. Does yours? Where does it go? Probably to something that's pleasant or of more interest.

Do you ever find your mind wandering when you're try-ing to meditate or pray? Of course you do. We engage in meditation or prayer with the best intentions. Our mind is so busy and active we look forward to a time of peace and quiet, a respite from too much brain activity. And we focus... for a minute or so. And then our mind takes off in another direction altogether.

As you become more aware of how your mind sabotages your good intentions to meditate on God's Word or spend ten minutes in concentrated prayer, you make a discovery. Your mind has "a mind of its own," so to speak. Regard-less of your good intentions to keep it under control and in balance, it still wanders away into thoughts about the past, future, pain or loss.[2]

As we use leashes and fences to keep our dogs where they should be, it may help to do the same with our thoughts. If you have a case of "the wandering thoughts," it will help to memorize these Scriptures and say them out loud to help control your thoughts when they threaten to wander into the wrong yard:

> Those who live according to the flesh have their minds set on what the flesh desires; but those who live in accordance with the Spirit have their minds set on what the Spirit desires (Romans 8:5).

> Do not conform to the pattern of this world, but be transformed by the renewing of your mind. Then you will be able to test and approve what God's will is—his good, pleasing and perfect will (Romans 12:2).

> With minds that are alert and fully sober, set your hope on the grace to be brought to you when Jesus Christ is revealed at his coming (1 Peter 1:13).

Ten Commandments
Part 1

Just imagine for a minute. What if dogs could create a list of ten commandments for their owners? Well, why not? There have been numerous spin-offs on the original Ten Commandments. I've seen ten commandments for husbands, wives, dogs, and cats. So why not for those of us who have dogs in our lives? (I hesitate to use the term "dog owners" because all too often the dogs own us. After all, don't we have to be home at certain times to feed and let our dogs out?)

So what would dogs write for us? Would the commandments be helpful or facetious? Would they be laughable or insightful? And how would they compare to the original Ten Commandments? Here is part of a suggested list by Richard Lederer:

I. Thou shalt remember that my life is likely to last ten to fifteen years. Any separation from you will be painful for me. Remember that before you adopt me.

II. Thou shalt give me time to understand what you want of me. Treat me kindly, my beloved friend, for no heart in the world is more grateful for kindness than this loving heart of mine.

III. Thou shalt place your trust in me. It is crucial to my well being.

IV. Thou shalt not be angry with me for long and shalt not lock me up as punishment. You have your work, your entertainment, and your friends. I have only you.

V. Thou shalt be aware that no matter how you treat me, I'll never forget it.[1]

Some people laugh when they read these, while others smile or chuckle or even cry. Did you catch the import of the five commandments? Go ahead and read them again. What did you read about your relationships with others? What biblical principles were suggested? Here are some things I "heard."

1. *Build your relationships on a permanent basis.* Rejection, especially after having a close relationship is very painful. Separation can occur physically but often emotional separation carries a greater pain. Ignoring loved ones or their overtures can be devastating. Not taking time to just "hang out" with your dog or a loved one falls under the separation or abandonment category. And it includes not listening. If there is a distance between you and someone else at this time, what can you do to move toward reconciliation?

2. *In your family, do you let others know exactly what you need or want from them or do they have to guess?* No creature, dog or human, is a mind reader. Be clear what you need. Communicate your needs as requests rather than demands. And above all, put into practice Ephesians 4:32: "Become useful and helpful and kind to one another, tenderhearted (compassionate, understanding, loving-hearted), forgiving one another [readily and freely], as God in Christ forgave you" (AMP, brackets in original). It may be helpful to ask yourself this question every day: "How will I demonstrate kindness today?"

3. *Do my family members and friends know I trust them?* If you were to ask your family members and friends, "In what way do I show you that I trust you?" what would their replies be? Another question to ask is, "In what ways do I demonstrate to you that I can be trusted?" Proverbs 11:13 says, "He who goes about as a talebearer reveals secrets, but he who is trustworthy and faithful in spirit keeps the matter hidden" (AMP).

4. *Do I deal with my anger constructively?* Scripture has much to say about the emotion of anger. Dealing with anger as soon as possible has merit, especially if it helps you relax, cool down, and act in a rational manner.

> He who is slow to anger has great understanding, but he who is hasty in spirit exposes and exalts his folly (Proverbs 14:29 AMP). This person actually suppresses strife in the beginning so it doesn't break out.

> He who is slow to anger is better than the mighty, he who rules his [own] spirit than he who takes a city (Proverbs 16:32 AMP, brackets in original).

> Good sense makes a man restrain his anger, and it is his glory to overlook a transgression or an offense (Proverbs 19:11 AMP).

> A [self-confident] fool utters all his anger, but a wise man holds it back and stills it (Proverbs 29:11 AMP, brackets in original). This verse means that the person does not give unbridled license to his anger but sort of hushes it up and puts it in the background. It also means that the anger is overcome.

> I [Nehemiah] was very angry when I heard their cry and these words. I thought it over and then rebuked the nobles and officials (Nehemiah 5:6-7 AMP, brackets in original).

The individual who practices and exerts self-control will find that his anger level actually decreases. He will not become as angry as if he were to simply cut loose with his first reaction. A calm consideration of the cause for the anger and the results will help you handle the situation properly.

Anger is a *secondary* emotion, and it's usually caused by fear, hurt, or frustration. (For more on anger see my book *Winning over Your Emotions*.)

5. *Do I say things I wish I hadn't?* Do you ever wish you hadn't said something or that you could take back some words? I sure do. Some of our words to others are difficult to erase.

> The words of the reckless pierce like swords, but the tongue of the wise brings healing (Proverbs 12:18).

> Whoever is patient has great understanding, but one who is quick-tempered displays folly (Proverbs 14:29).

> Better a patient person than a warrior, one with self-control than one who takes a city (Proverbs 16:32).

Ten Commandments
Part 2

In the previous reading, we covered the first five commandments. Here is a brief summary of some of the significant thoughts:

- Separations are painful for anyone.
- People and animals are grateful for kindness.
- Others as well as ourselves want to be trusted.
- Some have only one other significant person in their life. To whom are we significant?
- How we treat others leaves a lasting impression. The way we talk to our dogs and people is critical.

Here are the next two commandments dogs would have for their owners, according to Richard Lederer:

VI. Thou shalt talk to me sometimes. Even if I don't understand your words, I understand your voice when it's speaking to me. Speak to me often, for your voice is the world's sweetest music, as you must know by the fierce wagging of my tail whenever you greet me.

VII. Before hitting me, thou shalt remember that I have teeth that could easily crush the bones in your hand, but I choose not to bite you. Before beating me, know that patience and understanding will more quickly teach me the things you would have me learn.[1]

Again, let's look at each commandment one at a time.

6. *Talking is connecting.* The way we talk to our dogs or to people makes a difference. For most of us, our language changes according to the circumstances. We talk differently in formal situations than we do with family and friends. There's a special kind of language we use in talking with dogs. It's true! Do you know how it's different? When talking with adults, we usually use 10 to 11 words per sentence. When talking to dogs, we use around 4. We also use higher tones, distort words and phrases to make them less formal, and place more emphasis on our tone of voice.

When you talk to your dog, you're 20 times more likely to repeat or rephrase statements than when you're talking to a person. We also don't tell our dogs long stories or go on and on about a subject. (That's not to say we don't talk to them about our day sometimes.)

When it comes to excessive talking, some people drive us up a wall, especially if we tend to be sparse with our own words. Some people talk on and on, repeat what they've said, or do a combination of the two. Let's consider what the Word of God has to say about talking:

> Careful words make for a careful life; careless talk may ruin everything (Proverbs 13:3 MSG).

> If you want a happy, good life, keep control of your tongue, and guard your lips from telling lies (1 Peter 3:10 TLB).

Control of your tongue is not easy to accomplish in your own strength, but if you depend on the Holy Spirit for teaching and guidance, you will have help and strength far beyond your own.

When you talk to your dog or another person, every message has three components: 1) the content, 2) the tone of voice, and 3) the nonverbal communication. It's possible to use the same word, statement, or question and express many different messages simply by changing your tone of voice or body movement. Nonverbal communication includes facial expression, body posture, and gestures or actions.

Face-to-face communication generally consists of 7 percent content, 38 percent tone of voice, and 55 percent nonverbal communication. You're probably aware of the content of what you want to say, but perhaps you're not nearly as aware of your tone of voice. People have the capability of giving one sentence a dozen different meanings just by changing the inflections in the delivery. With people, be sure your words and tone match or they'll be confused by the mixed signals you're sending. One of the best ways to train your dog is to be aware of your tone of voice.

7. *A dog should never be struck.* Hitting a dog won't change his behavior, but it will cause him to look at you fearfully. Unfortunately, words can be as powerful as physical force when it comes to communicating with people. There are so many ways people beat up on each other verbally. All too often it's simply what we say and how we say it.

Scripture is clear that our words have tremendous power. They can heal, offer support and comfort, or cause great pain and harm. Here's what James had to say about the tongue:

> A bit in the mouth of a horse controls the whole horse. A small rudder on a huge ship in the hands of a skilled captain sets a course in the face of the strongest winds. A word out of your mouth may seem of no account, but it can accomplish nearly anything—or destroy it!
>
> It only takes a spark, remember, to set off a forest fire. A careless or wrongly placed word out of your mouth can do that. By our speech we can ruin the world, turn harmony to chaos, throw mud on a reputation, send the whole world up

in smoke and go up in smoke with it, smoke right from the pit of hell.

This is scary: You can tame a tiger, but you can't tame a tongue—it's never been done. The tongue runs wild, a wanton killer. With our tongues we bless God our Father; with the same tongues we curse the very men and women he made in his image. Curses and blessings out of the same mouth! (James 3:3-10 MSG).

As far as power is concerned, James compares the power of the tongue to the rudder of a ship. Comparatively speaking, a rudder is a small part of the ship, yet it can turn the ship in any direction and control its destiny. What you say to another person can turn your relationship in different directions. Criticism is often hidden under the camouflage of humor. When confronted about it, a person will attempt to avoid responsibility by saying, "Hey, I was just joking." That reminds me of a passage in the book of Proverbs: "Just as damaging as a madman shooting a deadly weapon is someone who lies to a friend and then says, 'I was only joking'" (26:18-19 NLT).

Faultfinding is a favorite pastime for many. Criticism is usually destructive, but it's interesting to hear those who criticize say they're "just trying to remold the other into a better person by offering 'constructive' criticism." All too often criticism doesn't construct. Instead, it demolishes. It doesn't nourish a relationship; it poisons it. Often the presentation is like this: "There is one who speaks rashly like the thrusts of a sword" (Proverbs 12:18 NASB). Destructive criticism accuses, tries to make the other person feel guilty, intimidates, and is often an outgrowth of personal resentment.

Instead of focusing on what annoys you, talk more about what you would *appreciate* the other person doing. Talking about what you don't like just reinforces the possibility of its continuance with even greater intensity. The principle of pointing another toward what you like conveys that you believe he or she is capable of doing what you've requested and accentuates the positive. If you do this consistently, along with giving praise and appreciation when the person complies, you will most likely see a change for the better.

I've also seen this principle work in the raising of our golden retriever named Sheffield. He was trained in the basics when he was four months old. He learned to bring in the paper, take items back and forth to my wife and me, bring the phone to me when it rang, and pick up items off the floor and put them in the trash. All it took was ignoring the times when he didn't do it right and giving praise and hugs when he did what I wanted. If I'd criticized him instead, I would have destroyed his spirit. And I don't think people are much different in this respect.

Ten Commandments
Part 3

Here are the last three of the ten commandments dogs would tell their owners, as suggested by Richard Lederer:

VIII. Before scolding me for being lazy or contrary, thou shalt ask thyself if something might be bothering me. Perhaps I am not getting the right food or I've been out in the sun too long or my heart is growing old and weak.

IX. Thou shalt take care of me when I get old. You, too, will grow old one day.

X. When the times comes for my final journey, thou shalt see that my trusting life is taken gently. I shall leave this earth knowing with the last breath I draw that you have loved me till the end. That is only fitting because you know how much I love you.[1]

Again, let's look at these in a little more depth.

8. *Don't scold or criticize—encourage instead.* Scolding or criticizing has a negative result. It's called discouragement. That's a condition we all like to avoid. It takes the heart right out of us. It's not a fun experience; rather, it's a state of misery. We can end up aching all over. Have

you been there? If you're human, you have. It's part of life, though we wish otherwise. What is discouragement? Looking at the word and taking it apart, we find the word "courage," with its root syllable *cou*. This is Latin for *heart*, which is the center of this condition. Discouragement is literally the "loss of heart." Many people around us are discouraged even though we may not be aware of it.

In some seasons of life, you may experience an overload of problems all at once. It's not that one of them by itself couldn't be handled, but put them all together and you feel overwhelmed. "It's too much," you say as you slip into a state of crisis. It's like the stereotypical western song where the singer laments that he lost his job, his girlfriend left him, his dog died, and now his truck won't run.

Instead of criticizing or offering "helpful comments," why not assume the role of "encourager"? Scripture says, "Watch the way you talk. Let nothing foul or dirty come out of your mouth. Say only what helps, each word a gift" (Ephesians 4:29 MSG). How can your words become a gift to each person? First, you need to have an attitude of optimism. The American Heritage Dictionary has one of the better definitions of "optimism": "a tendency or disposition to expect the best possible outcome, or to dwell on the most hopeful aspect of the situation." When this is your attitude or perspective, you'll be able to encourage others. Encouragement is "to inspire; to continue on a chosen course; to impart courage or confidence."

Encouragement takes work—constant, consistent work—for it to be effective. When you're an encourager, you're like a prospector or a deep-sea diver looking for hidden treasure. Every person has pockets of underdeveloped resources within. Your task is to search for these pockets, rejoice when you discover them, and then encourage and help the person expand them. What does the Word of God say about encouragement?

- When Apollos wanted to go to Achaia, the brothers and sisters encouraged him and urged him to go (Acts 18:27). You can do it! Go for it!

- "Encourage the timid and fainthearted" (1 Thessalonians 5:14 AMP). This means to console, comfort, and cheer up. We're to especially help the person who is ready to give up. Under "encourage," *Vine's Expository Dictionary of New Testament Words* defines the Greek word *paramutheomai*, translated "encourage" in this verse as "to stimulate [another person] to the discharge of the ordinary duties of life."

- We are to "bear one another's burdens" (Galatians 6:2; Ephesians 4:1-2; Colossians 3:13). "Bearing" means bringing ourselves next to another so he or she won't fail.

- "Encourage one another daily" (Hebrews 3:13). Here, "encourage" is associated with protecting believers from callousness.

- "Encouraging one another" (Hebrews 10:25). In this verse, "encouraging" means to keep someone on his feet who, if left on his own, would collapse.

- "Anxiety in a man's heart weighs it down, but an encouraging word makes it glad" (Proverbs 12:25 AMP).

If you follow these Scriptures, your life and the lives of others will be greatly enhanced.

We'll take a closer look at commandment IX in the next chapter.

Aging

Growing older happens to all living creatures, including dogs and humans. It pains us when we see a loved one die. Two of the worst days of my life were when two of my golden retrievers died, "Sheffield" and "Aspen I." I watched them age (I'm trying not to notice that I'm doing the same), and I loved them until the end.

Who ages best? Who desires the most from the experience of growing older? If we were to interview people about the ones they know who handled getting older gracefully, we'd probably hear comments like these:

- They've developed an accepting view of others and themselves; they're able to forgive shortcomings. They don't keep grudges.

- They're givers of their resources. They retain their passion to help others.

- They have concern about our world and the quality of the environment they will leave for the next generation.

- They're reflective; they continue to understand and learn about themselves as much as possible.

- They navigate their transitions well and grow through their experiences rather than getting stuck or regressing. They're willing to make changes within themselves and in their environment as best they can.

- They simplify as they age in order to derive the most out of life. They set and can accept limits.

- They're people of faith. Their relationship with God is essential.

- Others seek them out for their wisdom, counsel and insight.

- They persist in self-study, classes, seminars. They refuse to stagnate.

- Their lifestyle includes caring behaviors toward others and themselves. They've learned to take care of their bodies by eating well and exercising, and they can express their emotions genuinely.

- They are people of hope, not despair, even in the face of much loss.

- They have faced their mortality and accept that their death is coming.[1]

There are minuses that arrive as we age, yes, but there are certainly pluses also:

> You don't get old from living a particular number of years; you get old because you have deserted your ideals. Years wrinkle your skin, renouncing your ideals wrinkles your soul. Worry, doubt, fear and despair are the enemies which slowly bring us down to the ground and turn us to dust before we die.[2]

Growing older means detaching from the past, and it means attaching to the present and the future. It's making a decision to choose life now and a future that will last for eternity. As believers, our calling is not to treat aging as a disease to be prevented or treated or cured. God, the Giver of Life, doesn't indicate a normative lifespan or say that following Him and His guidance guarantees longevity. The more important question isn't how long we live but *how* we live.

Whether it's a person or our dog that is nearing death, we want them to know they are going to be loved up to the last moment of their existence on earth. As Christians, we have a different view of death than many:

> We avoid death or even fear it because death is an evil, the horrible rending of a person from her body, from loved ones, from the ability to be fully in God's image.
>
> Yet death is also a mercy, it is the final affliction of life's miseries. It is the entrance to life with God. Life's passing can be a beautiful gift of God. This riddle of death's evil and its blessing is not difficult to solve. We enact it every Good Friday as we recall the evil of Christ's death to be followed on Easter Sunday with the joy of his resurrection.[3]

As we reflect on our own journey of life, this question posed by Ken Gire is worthy of our consideration:

> The closer I get to the end of my life, [this] seems the only question that matters: Is the life I am living pleasing to God?
>
> The question will keep you up at nights. And it should. As we pull the covers to our chin and settle into our pillow, that's the question that should bring our day into the presence of God for His scrutiny. Did the life I lived today please You?
>
> How many things do we have to check off on our to-do list before we can say yes? How many questions…before we can be done with them all and drop off to sleep?
>
> Only one.
>
> Have I loved well?
>
> So it's the end of the day, and each of us is lying in our bed, reflecting. Have I loved well? Can it be heard in all my

conversations? Seen in my eyes? Felt when other people are in my presence? Was the truth I spoke today spoken in love? Were the decisions I made today based on love? Were my reactions? My devotions?

Have I loved well?

If we can answer yes to that question, it is enough.[4]

Now to address the last of Richard Lederer's 10 Commandments, looking at our final journey, read the next chapter, "What Do You See?"

What Do You See?

Do you have sunglasses? Most of us do. We usually don't select them with the same care we do with our prescription glasses because there are differences. Recently I read an article on the value of sunglasses for fishing, especially the use of polarization to eliminate glare. This caught my attention since fishing and dogs are my two favorite hobbies. When it comes to sunglasses, it's not a simple choice. The article described the differences and value of various colors of lenses. Some seem better than others for distinguishing the contrast between a rock and a bass. Seeing fish in the water is better with amber lenses rather than gray. I never knew that. One expert suggested that vermilion is the best all-around color of lens because it increases the contrast more than the colors themselves. It also blocks more blue light than gray, which helps with focusing and visual acuity. Once you read articles like this, you begin checking your old sunglasses—and then the prices of new ones (if you have prescription lenses, they're even more expensive). You can guess which ones I have now, and they have really helped me enjoy sight fishing.

Sight fishing is one of the ways to catch fish, especially bass. In a way, it's a combination of two sports: hunting and fishing. You're looking for a fish that at first you may not see. This involves stalking as well because you look for telltale signs, such as a shadow or a swirl in your search for a bass protecting its bed. You have to move carefully since bass notice the smallest movements.

When it comes to sight fishing from the shoreline, I've found the ultimate answer: Sheffield. That's right, Sheffield. What's a Sheffield? Remember, he was one of my golden retrievers. I used him as a bass spotter—a "shoreline sonar." I never intended to; it just happened.

In 1984, for our twenty-fifth wedding anniversary, my wife and I had our backyard redone to look like a mountain scene. It was a small area, but it had a couple of birch, two liquid amber trees, and one pine. We also put in some small ponds with a recirculating water-fall for sound and aeration. Only about 500 gallons of water were involved, but where there's water, there has to be fish, right? Well, there've been a variety over the years. In the small pond I raised trop-ical fish six months out of the year—usually fancy guppies. In the larger pond, we had crappie, a bluegill, and even a largemouth bass on occasion. Most of the time there were also two turtles and some leftover crawdads that I dropped in after fishing outings.

It didn't take Sheffield long to discover the critters. With no upland game birds to flush in the backyard, he decided the next best thing was stalking whatever was in the larger pond. I was amazed at his ingenuity and persistence. Often I would stand at the window and watch him. If I went outside and stood next to him, he kept looking for fish. If he couldn't see something clearly enough, he'd put his head beneath the surface of the water all the way up to his ears so he could get a better look. One day I decided to take a series of pictures of his stalking. I even attached a snorkel to his collar for effect. It looked just as though he were breathing through this appa-ratus when his head was submerged. Eventually I'd tell him, "Find the fish, Sheffield! Find the fish!" and he'd run to the pond and begin looking. I always wondered what he could see. How does the sight of dogs and people differ, if it does? So I did a bit of research. Here's some of what I discovered:

- People have an accurate perception of color. For instance, a person wearing a white shirt outside in the sunshine and then moving into a dark room will give the illusion the shirt has changed color, but we still know it's white.

- Our eyes are placed frontally, thus endowing us with very good binocular vision, which in turn allows us to focus well for short and long distances. At the same time, we have poor night vision and poor peripheral vision. The dog's sight is based on the needs of a predator—a visual field with a relatively large amount of binocular vision plus an additional monocular field for each eye, giving a total visual field of between 240 and 290 degrees. By comparison, ours has 180 degrees.

- Many parts comprise the eyeball, but of interest to us is the retina. The retina contains nerve cells called rods and cones. The rods are sensitive to light and the cones to color. Dogs have many rods and other reflective cells that are arranged in a layer that reflects incandescent light back to the receptor cells, hence magnifying its effect and allowing the dog to see well at dusk. Humans have three color sensitive cone cells: red, green, blue. Dogs only have two: green and blue. This means they can't distinguish red, green, and yellow objects based on color. However, they can still distinguish a red ball from a green one if there is a difference in the perceived brightness of the two.

- Dogs have poor vision up close, good vision at a distance, and excellent sensitivity to peripheral movement. However, the angle of vision varies between breeds. Breeds with lateral eye placement have better peripheral vision and poorer ability to focus straight ahead. The opposite applies to dogs with frontal eye placement.

- Most dog types can't focus on objects closer than about 25cm, but they are so good at detecting movement that an object may go unnoticed until it moves.

One day in the early spring I was walking the shoreline at Lake Arrowhead looking for smallmouth bass. I noticed Sheffield run out on a dock and then stop. When I caught up to him, he was staring into the water. Then I saw it as well—a bass. And it dawned on me. If he could spot them at home, why not here? And that's exactly how we fished. He had better sight than I did when it came to finding fish. So as we walked along I'd just say, "Find me a fish, Sheffield. Get me a fish." You should have seen his excitement when I landed a bass, let him sniff it, and then released it to catch another day! Yes, there is something to this sight fishing after all.

Speaking of seeing, that's what's involved in life as well. We need to keep our eyes open or we'll miss out on a lot of life. I've seen anglers so intent on fishing that they never notice the beauty of the foliage, trees, wildlife, or clouds. For me, the environment above the water is as important as what's underneath.

I've seen a husband so involved in what he was doing or thinking that he failed to notice his wife was wearing a new dress or had redecorated their bedroom. Or what about the wife who is so intent on what she's doing that she fails to notice her husband has fixed the broken light in the hall? None of those situations makes for a pleasant evening.

What do you see around you? Is there something important to look at, but you fail to notice? It happens. It's happened to me. Perhaps the intensity we give to such things as looking for fish should be directed elsewhere at times. Jesus had something to say about seeing: "Having eyes, do you not see?" (Mark 8:18 NASB). He also said, "I speak to them in parables; because while seeing they do not see" (Matthew 13:13 NASB). It's possible to see yet not get the message. It's possible to see yet not understand. That's what Jesus was concerned about. Life is more than what we notice here on earth. It's about a relationship with Jesus, our Lord and Savior. It's understanding who He is and what He taught, and then seeing life through His eyes, which eliminates much of the glare.

Saturated with the Word

Rainstorms vary. Some are like a persistent mosquito buzzing around and never going away. Some storms never amount to much, but you spend your day slipping your rain gear on and off, on and off. Other storms are intense. They soak. They drench. They create a soggy mess. Water oozes through every possible opening. Your clothes get wet, and soon your skin is moist. There isn't a dry inch on your entire body. This is total saturation.

Saturation is a positive thing when it comes to the Word of God. To live as a Christian in today's world, you've got to saturate yourself with God's Word. How do you do that? In war, "saturation bombing" was often used to obliterate enemy positions in certain areas. Planes continuously dropped load after load of bombs in a crisscross pattern until every inch of land had been covered. Similarly, as a follower of Christ, you need to allow the Holy Spirit to saturate every inch of your heart and mind with the truth of who you are and what you are becoming in Jesus Christ.

A number of years ago we raised shelties. Our male went by the name of Prince, and he lived up to it. He acted and walked like a regal. He thought the world revolved around him. He loved to ride in the car and, especially, the boat. One day I decided to take him with me to Lake Irvine. I enjoyed Prince's company because he didn't talk my ear off, wouldn't catch more fish than I would, and would agree with everything I said and wanted to do.

Prince was a beautiful dog with a rich, sable coat. Wherever he went, he drew people to him. We went to the lake and launched the boat, and as soon as we took off Prince went to the front of the boat and got on the bow. I was reminded of an ancient ship with a mast-head on the bow. Prince stood proudly, holding his head high and letting the wind ripple through his fur. I headed to the cove at full speed, and as I sped into the cover I suddenly changed my mind about fishing there, so I quickly swung the boat around and reversed my direction. My dog lost his balance and went flying into the lake. It was like he was launched from a catapult! I don't know which one of us was more surprised!

I swerved the boat around to where he was swimming (he wasn't too happy with me at that moment) and cut the motor. I picked him out of the water, but I didn't lift him into the boat right away because he was totally soaked. I held him away from the boat and gently squeezed his coat to eliminate most of the water. Only then did I bring him into the boat safe and sound.

My golden retriever is quite different from my sheltie. For one thing, he's four times heavier. As a retriever, he loves playing in the water, and his fur coat doesn't get soaked. In fact, it actually repels water. When he emerges from the water, he appears wet but the water hasn't penetrated very far into his thick fur. Within a short time, it looks as though he never went swimming.

Some of us are thick-coated like my retriever. God's truth has never thoroughly penetrated our outer layer to deeply influence us. We haven't been fully soaked in God or His Word. For growth to occur, we must saturate ourselves in God's truth. When I was a teenager, I spent a lot of time memorizing Scripture. The knowledge I gained helped more times than I can remember. On several occasions when facing a temptation or struggling with a decision, Scriptures came into my mind at the right moment. Usually it was 1 Corinthians 10:13 TLB:

> Remember this—the wrong desires that come into your life aren't anything new and different. Many others have faced exactly the same problems before you. And no temptation is

irresistible. You can trust God to keep the temptation from becoming so strong that you can't stand up against it, for he has promised this and will do what he says. He will show you how to escape temptation's power so that you can bear up patiently against it.

That message was a lifesaver for me as a young man. Unfortunately, throughout the decades of adulthood I didn't make a consistent effort to memorize God's Word. In 1995, however, a friend at family camp, Rick Hicks, shared a section from his new book *Seeking Solid Ground*, which is about Psalm 15. He gently challenged us to memorize this psalm because it explains how to get the most out of life and be close to God. I accepted the challenge. Memorization requires a bit more work for me these days, but by spending just two or three minutes each morning on it, the passage soon became mine. Now when I wake up at night I often quote Psalm 15 silently. I quote it when I'm driving. The words are reassuring. They keep me alert and on track for God. Why not give it a try?

> Who may worship in your sanctuary, LORD?
> Who may enter your presence on your holy hill?
> Those who lead blameless lives and do what is right,
>> speaking the truth from sincere hearts.
> Those who refuse to gossip
>> or harm their neighbors
>> or speak evil of their friends.
> Those who despise flagrant sinners,
>> and honor the faithful followers of the LORD,
>> and keep their promises even when it hurts.
> Those who lend money without charging interest,
>> and who cannot be bribed to lie about the innocent.
> Such people will stand firm forever (Psalm 15 NLT).

I've worked on many other passages since then. I don't want to stop! I encourage you to let God's Word shape your life. You'll never regret it. And the more you do, the more you'll want to do.

Oh, how I love [God's commandments]. I think about them all day long. They make me wiser than my enemies because they are my constant guide. Yes, wiser than my teachers, for I am ever thinking of your rules. They make me even wiser than the aged (Psalm 119:97-100 TLB).

Saturate—it will make a huge difference in your life.[1]

Loyalty and Faithfulness

The other day I was shocked as I looked through some of my books about collies that were written by Albert Paysen Terhune. Collies have always been one of my favorite breeds. I've owned a rough-coat collie and a Shetland sheepdog (sheltie). When a collie is mentioned, the picture that usually comes to mind is Lassie from the film or TV series. Actually, the classic *Lassie* film, which starred Elizabeth Taylor and was released in 1943, was based on a book written by Erick Knight. Unfortunately, that book wasn't based on a real dog.

There are many varieties of collies. "Collie" isn't a specific breed but a distinctive type of herding dog that originally came from Scotland and Northern England. Many of them are working herding dogs. I thought I had Terhune's entire collection of books until I searched the web and discovered that between the years 1896 and 1961, he'd authored more than 65 of them!

Within his fascinating *A Book of Famous Dogs*, Terhune talks about dogs from ancient days, dogs owned by great authors, dogs of kings, dogs in the theater, and dogs of war. One of the chapters that captured my attention, probably because I work with those who experience grief and trauma, was on dogs who appeared to be "professional mourners."

In Edinburgh, Scotland, there is a cemetery in a churchyard that has a statue of what appears to be a shabby and shaggy dog. This statue is in honor of Greyfriars Bobby, the best known and best loved occupant in the cemetery. At the bottom of the statue was a drinking fountain for animals.

In 1858, a farmer named Gray died. When his body was taken by cart to the graveyard, a nondescript dog trotted along under the cart. Once his master was buried, the dog lay mournfully on top of the grave. No amount of coaxing could entice him to leave. He stayed there motionless through inclement weather and the hunger that he must have felt. Nothing would make him leave his vigil. Greyfriars loyalty toward his master was so strong that he stayed until the church custodian drove him away. But as soon as he could, he returned to watch over his master's grave. Once again the custodian chased him away. Then one of the gravediggers told the custodian how the dog had followed his master's cart for miles to the cemetery. The dog and his master had been inseparable, and even though the farmer had left, his dog wasn't about to leave him. The custodian let the pup stay after that.

Some people brought the animal food and water. His devotion became a topic of conversation in the small town. More and more people came to see him, bringing him food and scraps from their tables. Someone brought cloth to make a bed for him. Some tried to lure him away from the grave, but Greyfriars was committed. Stories were written about him, and people from other countries came to see him. Artists came to paint him, but nothing seemed to faze him or dissuade him from his loyal vigil. He continued to stay year after year. Fourteen years after the death of his master, Greyfriars Bobby didn't wake up one morning. He had died while watching over his master's grave.[1]

The story of this dog has been told and retold scores of times in articles and books. In 1961, Walt Disney produced a movie about him. But there are so many other stories about the loyalty of dogs for their owners. What an amazing example of steadfastness God has given us through his creation of the dog.

After almost 50 years of counseling individuals and couples, I wish I'd met more people who had such an intense level of commitment and loyalty. That small dog really did nothing physically spectacular or outstanding or newsworthy, but he was faithful. Nothing led him astray whether it was discomfort, or pain, or enticement, or something better.

Think about loyalty for a minute. What does it mean to you? Perhaps it means people can count on your word or they can count on you doing what you say you'll do. It can mean you'll be there for others during their difficult times. It's one thing for a dog to be loyal but so much better when it's a quality in our own life. God's Word says:

> He who pursues righteousness and loyalty finds life, righteousness, and honor (Proverbs 21:21 NASB).

> A faithful man will abound with blessings (Proverbs 28:20).

> I delight in loyalty rather than sacrifice, and in the knowledge of God rather than burnt offerings (Hosea 6:6 NASB).

Loyalty has many synonyms, including faithfulness, allegiance, devotion, steadiness, trust, and reliability. Here are some questions to consider.

Faithfulness: Who exhibits this toward you?
                Who sees you as faithful toward them?

Allegiance: Who exhibits this toward you?
                Who sees you as a dependable partner or friend?

Devotion: Who exhibits this toward you?
                Who sees you as devoted toward them?

Steadiness: Who exhibits this toward you?
                Who sees you as steady, especially in your faith?

Trust: Who exhibits this toward you?
                Who sees you as trustworthy?

Reliability: Who exhibits this toward you?
                Who sees you as reliable?

How can you be more loyal in your relationships? You may not have a statue created in your honor and memory, but God has much more planned for you when you follow His Word.

Chewing Is Not a Spiritual Gift

I went to a doggy boutique the other day, but not on purpose. My dogs were groomed so I had to go in and pick them up. Some dogs would be embarrassed by all the frilly clothes and stuff that was available. *People* buy this stuff for their pets. It's certainly not something dogs would pick out—or at least my dogs! I did see one item that made sense. It was a bandana to put around a dog's neck. On it were the words "Born to Chew." Yes! That's so true. Dogs have a built-in gene that drives them. For puppies, if it moves, they chew it. If it's bright, they chew it. If it doesn't move, they chew it. Puppies (and even some older dogs) train us to put things away, close doors, close the lid on the toilet, and never leave anything around we don't want gnawed on or eaten. Puppies are great teachers. They change our lives as we learn to be on the alert, watch where we leave things, watch where they're off to, and watch where we walk (especially before they're potty-trained).

When we bought our first sheltie, we discovered the true meaning of the word "chew." We left Prince home with a dog sitter—one of my graduate students. A couple of days after we left, I called home to see how everyone was doing. Mike said after a hesitant pause, "Well, we're doing okay. Prince chewed the corner off my leather suitcase this morning."

"Oh, I'm sorry," I replied, not sure what else to say.

I called home a couple of days after that.

"Hey, Mike, what's going on?" Again there was a hesitant pause.

"Well, Norm, I've been sitting here pasting pieces of my thesis back together after Prince chewed it up this morning."

"Oh!" I said. Now I really didn't know what to say!

Our first golden retriever taught his dog sitter a few things, one of which was "never leave three dozen freshly baked cookies on the counter within reach and then go outside—even for a minute." This happened, and Sheffield really enjoyed himself. Unfortunately, the flour, sugar, and chocolate chips, which are toxic to dogs, churned and fermented in his stomach all night. In the morning the vet taught Sheffield the meaning of bingeing and purging. It wasn't a pretty sight. We also had some early American furniture that was modified to a new style—distressed. That too wasn't a pretty sight.

Since I'm writing about dogs and their chewing, I decided to go to the source—a dog—and interview him about this tendency so I could avoid speculation. I talked to one of my goldens.

"Shadow, why do you dogs chew so much—especially when you're puppies?"

"I love to chew! It's sheer heaven to sink my teeth into shoes, furniture, rolled-up newspapers, wall corners, broom handles, you name it, I'll gnaw on it. It *feels soooo* good! I discovered the joy of chewing as a puppy when my teeth were coming in. I lost all of my 28 baby teeth just like you lost all 20 of your baby teeth. When I was about four months old, my permanent teeth started to come in, so I needed to chew on something. My desire to chew skyrocketed.

"Say, if you know someone who has a puppy, please tell him or her to not yell at the pup. The poor critter is just trying to ease the pain of new teeth growing in. He'd really appreciate it if his owner occasionally rubbed ice cubes on his gums. That helps while teething, just like it does for human babies. The numbness eases the pain, which in turn lessens the desire to sink teeth into that messy pile of clothes and shoes on the floor of closets.

"By the time dogs are about six months old, the tooth fairy is through visiting but we haven't given up our love for chewing. So the next time you discover our teeth marks on something of yours, please understand that chewing is a great pleasure in life. Why not give pups something you want them to chew on?"

"Why do you chew on my shoes?"
"I need to chew on something. If you'll supply chew toys, that would go a long way to protect your possessions. Better yet, a bone from the butcher really hits the spot! Nothing satisfies my craving to chew more than a good bone."

My other dog, Aspen, jumped into the conversation.

"You may think I chew your things to get back at you. You probably think I'm upset because you leave me home alone during the day. Feel guilty if you want, but that's not the case. If you don't believe me, look it up. Research shows I don't chew out of spite. Sure, I get stressed when you leave me alone. The first half hour is the worst. I think the technical term for it is 'separation anxiety.' I may chew on your stuff out of anxiety, boredom, or just for fun. I do have a confession. I love it when you feel guilty. I've noticed that the more guilt you feel, the more attention and treats I get when you return home. So even though your guilt is unnecessary, it usually works out well for me."

Shadow cut back in to add one last word of advice about chewing and eating.

"If you're a chocolate lover, you may be shocked, but the rumors are true. Chocolate is very bad for us dogs. It can trigger seizures and even kill us. It's the chemicals in cocoa that put me in danger."

"Yes," I said. "Theophylline, theobromine, and menylethylamine. The purer the chocolate, the more dangerous it is."

"That's right," Shadow said. "A couple of bites of a Milky Way bar probably won't hurt me, but rich Godiva chocolates or even some of that chocolate people use for baking can mean danger and death. So please keep it away from me and my friends. We tend to wolf down almost anything, whether it's good for us or not."

Puppyhood is a time of enjoyment, laughter, and teaching. Wise owners find out as much as they can about what it takes to own dogs, and not just in terms of money. Dogs require a lot of time and energy too. It will be a time of character building—for you as an owner. There are certain character qualities that will need to be developed, including patience and responsibility. When one of my dogs ate something or chewed up some item, I learned to turn the blame around to the one responsible—usually me. If they chewed it, I probably left it out. I learned to close doors, drawers, and put items out of their reach. Puppyhood can trigger anger and irritation, but your pup doesn't deserve to bear the brunt of it. Consider these thoughts:

> He who is slow to anger is better than the mighty, he who rules his [own] spirit, than he who captures a city (Proverbs 16:32 NASB).

> A [self-confident] fool utters all his anger, but a wise man holds it back and stills it (29:11 AMP, brackets in original).

Your puppy needs your patience and gentle correction. Doesn't that sound like what we need as well? God is patient with us, and He does provide correction:

> All Scripture is God-breathed and is useful for teaching, rebuking, correcting and training in righteousness (2 Timothy 3:16).

Whoever heeds life-giving correction will be at home among the wise. Those who disregard discipline despise themselves, but the one who heeds correction gains understanding (Proverbs 15:31-32).

Whoever loves discipline loves knowledge, but whoever hates correction is stupid (12:1).

The Word "Dog"

Do you know that there are approximately 79 million dogs in the United States, and more than 1 in 3 American families own a dog (or a dog owns them)? Roger Caras said, "Dogs are not our whole life, but they make our lives whole." Can you imagine a language or vocabulary without the word "dog"? I can't.

Let's take a look at how we use the word "dog." What do you call someone who is tenacious? A bulldog. If you're fortunate or a show-off, you're called a "lucky dog." In 1150, St. Bernard of Clairvaux coined the phrase, "Love me, love my dog" which is an expression of unconditional affection. What does the phrase "dog-eared" relate to? Books that are used so extensively that someone has folded down the corners of quite a few pages so they look like the ear of a dog. Do you eat hot dogs?

In the nineteenth-century some people were concerned that sausages were made from dog meat, as evidenced by this popular rhyme:

> Oh where, oh where has my little dog gone?
> Oh where, oh where can he be?
> Now sausage is good, baloney, of course.
> Oh where, oh where can he be?
> They make them of dog, they make them of horse.
> I think they make them of he.[1]

When one hot sausage vendor noticed his customers needed a lot of napkins, he started putting his sausages in bread—and hot dogs as we know them were born.

Sometimes the word "dog" shows up in places or has an influence that may seem strange. Take the Canary Islands, for example. When you hear about them, what do you assume? That there must be canaries there, and that's how the islands got their name. But that's not true. The canaries, which are there, were named after the islands, and the islands were named after the large dogs that were found there. When the Romans came to the Canary Islands they encountered not only fierce natives, but also their dogs. The Latin word for dog is *canis*, and they named one of the islands "Canaria" because of these dogs. *Canis* is also where we get the word "canine."[2]

Have you ever been in the doghouse? Perhaps not literally, but most of us have at some time or the other. We know what it means—that we're in trouble for some reason.

Have you had days where you put in a great deal of work, but for some reason you don't seem to accomplish much? Perhaps you discovered you made a mistake, and that's why there weren't many results. You felt like you were "barking up the wrong tree." That's a phrase that means wasting energy by taking the wrong path. It's been around a long time and was created to describe a pack of hunting dogs who crowded around the base of a tree barking their heads off thinking they had treed a coon…but the raccoon was long gone.

If I mentioned the phrase "Three Dog Night," you may think of the singing group from the 1970s. That's not the case. A "three-dog night" has to do with the weather. If the weather is slightly cold, it would take one dog's body heat to keep you warm at night. If it's colder, it might be a two-dog night. Really cold and freezing means you need three dogs to create enough body heat to feel comfortable.

I've always wondered about the popular phrase "it's raining cats and dogs." Here's one explanation I found:

There are a number of [possible] explanations. Dogs and cats were closely associated with the rain and wind in northern mythology. Dogs were often pictured as the attendants of Odin, the storm god, and cats were believed to cause storms. Another theory was that during heavy rains in seventeenth-century England, some city streets became raging rivers of filth carrying many drowned cats and dogs. But the more simple explanation is cats and dogs make a lot of noise when they fight—"fighting like cats and dogs"—so they have become a metaphor for a noisy rain or thunderstorm.[3]

This is a test of sorts. Let's see if you know what these phrases mean. I'll give you a hint. They all pertain to a dog in some way.

- A person who aggressively seeks out the media to get attention.
- A piece of cornbread hunters share with their dogs.
- To put on airs or make a flashy display of him- or herself.
- An expression to describe a golf fairway that has an angle to it.
- A small tent that is considered more appropriate for children than adults.
- The hot days of summer. The phrase originated with the Romans because a certain star rose and set in conjunction with the sun, and they believed this caused the increase in heat.
- A special way of swimming.[4]

I discovered more than 400 references to dogs in our current American English vernacular. As you can see, the word "dog" has made our language more colorful. When we use that or similar words, most people know what we mean.

Another word that has permeated our vocabulary and should have a clear meaning is the word "Christian." We use this word to denote someone is a follower of Jesus Christ. And if we hear that a person is a Christian, we have certain expectations of what he or she believes and how the person acts. We expect Christians to follow the teachings of the Bible. Some do, but some don't. We expect Christians to reflect a certain belief system as well as a lifestyle. We expect them to be different in what they do in comparison to others in our society. Scripture says:

> We know that we have come to know him if we keep his commands. Whoever says, "I know him," but does not do what he commands is a liar, and the truth is not in that person. But if anyone obeys his word, love for God is truly made complete in them. This is how we know we are in him: Whoever claims to live in him must walk as Jesus did (1 John 2:3-6).

Scripture is quite clear about how we are to respond if we follow Jesus. The bottom line is this: Is our behavior consistent with what we say, what we know, and what we believe? The word "Christian" means "little Christ." Do we really reflect this? It's something to think about.

Lost

Have you ever been lost? Most of us have at some time. Sometimes it's when we're driving. I've even been lost when I had a GPS in the car. Being lost is not a comfortable feeling because we're out of control. Sometimes we panic. And yet sometimes we don't even know we're lost!

When I was five or six, my family went to Ensenada, Mexico, to do some fishing. We stayed at a motel, and one afternoon I disappeared (or so my parents told me much later). The story goes that I'd noticed some people fishing on the rocks for eels. To a young boy, this looked great so I took off and climbed out on the rocks to witness the excitement. Well, back in the hotel was another form of excitement—panic on the part of my parents. "Norman is missing. He's lost!" my parents exclaimed. My older brother joined the search, and after a while he found me. He said, "Everyone is upset and thought you were lost." I told him, "I wasn't lost. I knew right where I was the whole time."

Dog owners experience the same kind of panic when their dogs go missing. Years ago we raised shelties, and one time we gave five puppies away to our friends. Samson was one of the pups. He was a typical sheltie—energetic, noisy, and loved to run and play. He loved Don and Billie, his owners, and followed them around the yard. Shelties seem to have a built-in "fetch the ball" gene. Samson's only problem was that he had another built-in gene called "roam." He loved to get out and wander the neighborhood for miles and miles. He also had an intense dislike for the UPS truck. When it came and he could escape, he would bark at it and chase it for blocks. Samson's roam gene got him lost quite often, although I'm sure he would say as I did as a child, "I'm not lost. I know exactly where I am."

On one of his many escapades, Samson found a park. It was great—acres of grass, lots of tall trees, bushes, and smells…oh, the smells. It was dog heaven. As he investigated the smells, he came across one he decided to follow. It led him to a clump of bushes, and when he stuck his nose in he encountered a large raccoon. These animals may be cute to people, but they can be vicious with their pointed teeth and razor-sharp claws. The raccoon did a number on Samson. Half dead, he crawled away. In the morning someone found him and took him to the local humane society.

Don and Billie searched for Samson as soon as they realized he was gone. They drove to areas where he'd been found before, but there was no trace of him. Billie finally decided to go to the humane society. She looked through the various kennels and then came to Samson. His hair was matted, his eyes were glazed, and he looked like he was in a stupor. He had an incision from shoulder to hip and many stitches across his chest. She called his name but received no response. Billie left, believing this wasn't Samson. She told her husband about the dog, and he asked, "Are you sure it wasn't Samson? Perhaps we should look again." So they returned, and as soon as they approached the kennel he was right there to greet them. On Billie's first visit he'd been groggy from the anesthesia he'd received for his surgery.[1]

Samson, who was lost, was found! If you've never lost a dog, it's hard to imagine the feeling of relief Don and Billie felt when they'd found their dog.

Because of hurricane Katrina, losses abounded—homes, cars, a culture, people, and pets. So much was lost; and so very little recovered. Such was the case with Martha, who lived in a small, older house in the Ninth Ward of New Orleans with her small dog, Fritz. One night the waters of the hurricane swept through aided by multiple breaks in the levee. The floodwaters rose faster than any-one could imagine. Rescue workers in a boat came to Martha's house and moved her to safety. But in the panic, Fritz was left behind. A few hours later it dawned on Martha that Fritz hadn't been rescued, as was the case with thousands of animals in the area. Not only did Martha lose her home and belongings, but also her only remaining family member. Her sorrow was intense.

Six weeks later Martha stopped by our hurricane relief chaplain headquarters at the edge of the Ninth Ward. She wondered if some-one would take her back to what was left of her home and help her find Fritz's remains so she could bury him. The director of the Victim Chaplain's group said he would be happy to assist. They arrived, went up to the front door, opened it, and walked in. Then they heard the sound—a weak woof coming from the bathroom. Looking at one another in shock, they opened the door of the bathroom and there stood Fritz, skin and bones on legs barely able to hold him up. He'd existed on water and chewing anything edible in the confines of that room. He was just hours away from death, so they rushed him to the vet. IVs were started immediately. Today Martha doesn't have her old home, but she does have something important—Fritz.[2]

This ending is similar to a story in the New Testament about a father and a son. Often known as the story of the Prodigal Son, it's about a son who takes his inheritance early and sets off to live a life of excess. When the money runs out and the son is out of work, he returns home, hoping to ask his father for work as a hired servant. But the father meets him at the road and exclaims, "This son of mine was dead and is alive again; he was lost and is found" (Luke 15:24).

God rejoices when we stop our wandering, when we realize how He sees us and loves us so we return to Him. We never have to feel lost again if we remember that God sought us out and redeemed us because He loves us and wants to spend time with us.

The Touch of the Master

You're out walking your dog in public. He's on a leash and well behaved (hopefully you are too!). You stop and he sits down. Soon a person comes up, looks at your dog, and then at you and says...

Now, what is the first statement most people say in this situation? "Does he bite?" or "What's its name?" More than likely it will be, "May I pet him?" That's our first inclination when we see a beautiful dog—to run our hands through his fur. We like the feel on our hands.

Most people don't realize the health benefits people receive from petting dogs. It has a calming effect on us, and it lowers our blood pressure, our heart rates, and calms us down if we're stressed. And the benefits go both ways. There is a program called the Tellington TTouch Method (TTouch), which is used to influence the behavior and character of dogs as well as enhance their ability to learn. Its purpose is to improve and maintain the quality of a dog's life. There are different points on the dog's body to touch with specific types of touches. This training is designed to reduce fear, pain, and stress for the animal.

One specific area is called the ear touch. It's one of the most effective ways of calming a hyperactive dog. It's also used in cases of shock to stabilize circulation. You gently stroke the dog's ear with your thumb from the center of the head to the base of the ear and all the way to the tip of the ear. You're not pulling the ear; just stroking the entire length of the ear gently. To help a dog relax, use slow, gentle slides on his ear.[1]

Part of the ministry provided by therapy dogs is the sense of touch. When a person is in a nursing home, rehabilitation center, or hospital and they see a therapy dog approach, they usually want to touch or hug the animal. Several years ago my publisher was rereleasing one of my earlier books about dogs at a large booksellers convention. Since the location was on the East Coast, I didn't take my dog with me. The publisher arranged for what I called a "rent-a-dog." The golden retriever came equipped with a trainer. As we walked through the convention hall, we ran into Joni Erickson Tada, who is a quadriplegic and has a wonderful ministry for the disabled. We wanted to talk, but she had an appointment across the hall so she asked us to follow her. When we arrived, the first thing she did was undo her arm from its position on her chair and place it on the head and back of our dog. The delight on her face was a gift. I'm not sure how much she could really feel, but she still wanted to touch and connect with the dog.

A friend of mine has a therapy dog with a unique ministry. Bucky visits the terminally ill. The people know they are dying, and they find the presence of this dog a source of comfort. One patient who had both feet and most of her fingers amputated had Bucky on her bed with her for more than an hour every day. She said at one point that his presence and comfort gave her the encouragement to go on.

There is one touch that most dogs want more than any others, and that is a touch from his master. One of my goldens pursues me in the evening for those touches and moans his delight as I comply. He never seems to get enough of my attention.

You and I are the same as our dogs. We long for touch. It may be from a parent, or a spouse, or child, or friend, or God Himself. We can't exist without being touched. One of the worst traumas of life is that of neglect, which happens to many children in orphanages in many third-world countries. The babies lie in their cribs 23 hours a day starving for love and interaction. Unfortunately, sometimes neglect occurs in our homes too. Some people feel as though they're untouchable, which drives them to despair.

In the New Testament, there are numerous stories of Jesus—how

He touched people and how people touched Him. The Gospels especially are full of stories about people who sought to touch Jesus: little children, a woman suffering from hemorrhages who desperately grasped the hem of His garment, a prostitute who anointed Jesus' feet with her tears and wiped them with her hair, and even the disciple Thomas, who because of his doubt said he wouldn't believe unless he could feel Jesus' wounds with his own hands. In those days, there were many who were considered untouchable because of diseases and being ceremonially unclean. Jewish law at that time was clear. Lepers were untouchable; and people were afraid to touch them because of contagiousness. We think now how terrible that was, but for a long time many people in our own time felt the same about people who had AIDS. We live in a culture that often says "Don't touch" in many situations, be it at church or in a shop. John Ortberg, in his book *Love Beyond Reason*, wrote:

> The leper made no attempt to touch Jesus. The leper understood the situation. He knew the law.
>
> But notice what Jesus did: "Moved with pity, Jesus stretched out his hand and touched him, and said to him, 'I do choose. Be made clean!'"
>
> …Jesus did not need to touch the leper to cleanse him. He performed other miracles at a distance; all he had to do was "say the word." The word healed his body, but the touch healed his soul. But Jesus wanted something understood.
>
> The miracle of the touch is that Jesus was willing to share another person's suffering in order to bring about healing. This is a foreshadowing of the cross: Jesus taking on our sin so that we could take on his life. By his stripes we are healed.
>
> In a contagious world, we learn to keep our distance. If we get too close to those who are suffering, we might get infected by their pain. It may not be convenient or comfortable. But only when you get close enough to catch their hurt will they be close enough to catch your love.

Jesus did not call his followers to live in quarantine...

God's shop is full of signs that say please touch. We may not want to. We are afraid or shy or busy. But it is only when people are touched in their brokenness that healing comes.

Today there will be people in your work waiting for someone to touch them. Will you be the one? Put an arm around the shoulder of a friend. Take the hand of someone who hurts. Embrace a child. Please touch.[2]

Yes, your dog needs to be touched. Your family and friends need your touch. But more than that, you and I need to be touched by our Master. He's always present, so ask Him to draw near. You will experience a touch that can sustain, encourage, comfort, and even bring healing. His touch will assure you that you are loved.

Your Pedigree

Do you have a pedigree? Yes, you do whether you realize it or not. Does your dog? Yes. Does your dog care? Doubtful. I've never seen a group of dogs sitting around talking about their ancestors and whether their bloodlines and ancestry were pure or not. They don't seem to look at mixed breeds (mongrels or mutts) with contempt or shun them because they're not purebreds. Unfortunately some people do. They are hung up on their ancestry and whether they came from the "right" stock or not. They believe that being one nationality or having a great-great uncle who was a third cousin twice removed to a president makes them special.

Most Americans, at least, are of mixed ancestry, and we like it. I'm part German, part English, and a small part Native American. I admit I value the Native American part more than the other parts. Only recently I discovered which Native American tribe or nation I came from. People like to know their history; dogs couldn't care less. Another dog is just another dog to them. Some people care about their dogs' lineage. I've heard many talk about their dogs' pedigree or the fact their pups are purebred. This can be heard especially at dog shows, where many owners carry their dogs' pedigrees with them to whip out and show to everyone who is or isn't interested.

What is a "pedigree"? The word comes from an Old French phrase that means "foot of the crane." Why this phrase? The clawlike, three-branched mark that was used in genealogical charts resembled the

foot of this bird. Pedigrees didn't originate with dogs or other animals, but with us. That's right, people established the importance of
pedigrees. Then they extended the importance to their animals. My
last two British shorthair cats happened to have extensive, purebred
pedigrees.

Let's take a look at some purebred dogs with pedigrees. Some are
known for their looks, some for their temperament, and others for
their abilities.

In the dog world, who is considered the smartest? The general
consensus is the border collie, the golden retriever, and the standard
poodle.

One of the assumptions about poodles is that they came from
France. They did originate in Europe and were used as hunting dogs.
The common coat clip for poodles shows them sheared around their
hindquarters. This was done because their thick coats were a problem in water and thick brush. This practice continues to the present
time, but in most cases it's to achieve the standard look for the breed.

Where did Chihuahuas get their name? From the state in Mexico
where they were discovered. And what they lack in size, they make up
in longevity. That breed generally lives the longest of the dogs.

When you hear the name Saint Bernard, what picture comes to
mind? For many, it's a large, two- or three-colored dog with a brandy
cask around its neck for rescuing someone in the snow. That concept
is so farfetched. This image came from some paintings done in the
eighteenth century. No one in their right mind would give someone
suffering from hypothermia some form of alcohol.

What dogs are considered the best swimmers? One breed is the
gentle, giant Newfoundland. They are top swimmers and are often
trained for water rescues. Their coats are water resistant, and they
have webbed feet for swimming. Not all dogs like water, nor do all
dogs swim. One of these is the basset hound which means "rather
low." That description is fitting because they have long bodies but
very short legs.

Some breed names don't mean what they seem to imply. An

example is the greyhound. The "grey" is not for the color but comes from an Old Norse word that means "female." Greyhounds are fast; they can reach speeds up to 45 miles per hour!

Perhaps some of the emphasis on dog pedigrees originated because certain types of dogs were associated with royalty. Bloodhounds were originally owned by royalty, and the word "blooded" means "aristocratic." I found this entry in *A Treasury for Dog Lovers*:

> Pekinese were the exclusive property of the ancient Chinese Imperial Court and guarded the emperors. Chinese royalty carried Pekinese puppies in the huge sleeves of their robes. The common people had to bow to the Pekinese. The dogs also wore silk robes and had their own staffs to groom and care for them—that's going a bit overboard. How this little dog guarded is beyond me. (Although I remember when I was about 3 or 4 one lived next door. I came up to him and petted him when he was eating—wrong move—and he jumped up and bit me on the lip.)
>
> Lhasa apsos were originally bred as guard dogs in Lhasa, Tibet, more than two thousand years ago. The first Lhasa apsos in the United States were gifts from the thirteenth Dalai Lama in the 1930s.
>
> Akitas possess a double coat, with a dense straight undercoat and a thick outer coat. This coat makes the dog waterproof, as well as being well equipped for the fierce winters in northern Japan. Akitas came to the United States in 1937, when Helen Keller visited Japan and received one as a gift.[1]

Since most breeds come from other countries, do we in the United States have any homegrown ones we can claim? How about the Boston terrier? Nope. It's a cross between the English bulldog and now extinct English white terrier.

Who really cares about pedigrees anyway? We don't look at a pedigree first and then decide to love our dogs. Or do you? I sincerely doubt it. And what about our own pedigrees? It's been given to us not by our parents but by God. *He* is our maker. *He* gives us value. In His eyes we're prized as being purely for Him. To Him we are super special regardless of our nationalities, color, size, or abilities. We are someone because of Him. I believe God says to all of us:

> You are My creation, My handiwork, My masterpiece. I'm so proud of what I've done. I see Myself in you and talk about who you are to the angels all the time. Humankind is still discovering the intricacies of the human body. I carefully put together every fiber of your being to show the world My excellence and My majesty. I've put a spirit in you that will live forever and ever. This is something no human mind will ever fully grasp.
>
> Give praise to Me, My daughter, My son, for the wonders I've performed in designing your every part. Take care that you do not compare yourself to anyone but Me. That's right! And I'll tell you why. I made you just the way I wanted you, and I made you with your own limitless potential, just as I am eternal. Therefore, continually set your sights on the greatness of who I am. Stand tall, My child. No other creature in the universe compares to you!

This is our pedigree. We don't need anything else.

> You [LORD] created my inmost being; you knit me together in my mother's womb. I praise you because I am fearfully and wonderfully made; your works are wonderful, I know that full well (Psalm 139:13-14).

> Before I formed you in the womb I knew you, before you were born I set you apart; I appointed you as a prophet to the nations (Jeremiah 1:5).

> Just as [God] chose us in Him before the foundation of the world, that we would be holy and blameless before Him. In

love He predestined us to adoption as sons through Jesus Christ to Himself (Ephesians 1:4 NASB).

I always pray with joy…being confident of this, that he who began a good work in you will carry it on to completion until the day of Christ Jesus (Philippians 1:6).

Guard Dog or Guard Your Dog?

Some people want a dog for protection. They feel safer when there's one on the premises. Some want a dog who loves everyone in their family but will protect them from everyone else. Some guard dogs are chosen because of their reputation, breed, size, and even ugliness. (Yes, ugly! In fact, there's a national competition for the ugliest dog every year.) Where did the idea of guard dogs originate?

Two police dogs, which pursue and apprehend lawbreakers, were first used in Germany in the late 1800s. The German shepherd was the first choice, followed by the Airedale terrier and the Doberman pinscher. Since then, in various parts of the world, other breeds have been used. A well-trained police dog can make patrol work much more efficient and effective. Sometimes the very sight of a dog prevents a crime from occurring.

Dogs do make excellent sentries. The German spitz has been a traditional guard in Germany, the Dutch Smoushond protects stables. The Keeshonden is used to watch over houseboats in Belgium and Holland. Today, guard dogs work in all sorts of places—prisons, nuclear energy plants, military installations, museums, and historical sites, including the Statue of Liberty.[1]

Often we think of breeds such as pit bulls and rottweilers as the ideal guard dog as well. Some breeds have been bred for just that purpose. My son-in-law is a city fireman, and I've done ride-alongs with him. Most of the calls are medical alerts rather than fires. On one such call in a rough section of town, we drove down the street and it appeared that every other house had a guard dog—all pit bulls! We arrived at the destination, walked up to the gate, and stopped. There he was—stocky, big, and staring at us. The firemen and I wondered what was going on in the dog's mind because his face was expressionless. Was he thinking, "Here comes lunch" or "The chubby one looks good to me. He'll be slow"? We looked at each other, and one fireman said, "Let's walk in together. He can't get all of us. We'll just sacrifice someone. Norm—you're the oldest, you go first." *Great!* I thought.

We opened the gate and all four of us walked toward the house. The dog kept sitting, and then he stood. He took two steps toward us, and we hesitated. He "smiled" and wagged his tail until it looked like it would fall off! He acted like he hadn't had any attention in a month. That dog taught us that looks and stereotypes can be deceiving, and each dog is unique. We were able to go into the house and provide the needed aid to the resident while a happy, friendly dog received some needed attention.

Guard dogs come in all sizes. Some dogs are "alert" dogs. My golden retrievers qualify for this task. They'll hear noises I never hear and give one or two barks. By the tone and pattern, I know something is up. My dogs are alert dogs—yes—but guard dogs—no. Any intruders would be in danger of being licked to death. Some of the toy dog varieties are also excellent alert dogs. What about your dog? Is he or she helpful to alert you? Will your pup guard you or your possessions?

Let's turn this around. How are you at guarding your dog? Yes—your dog needs guarding. The best way to guard your dog is not to cure a problem or illness but protect and prevent. It's less costly. Every animal owner needs access to a good vet, and because of the cost, you might even consider having a medical plan. That's right, a medical plan for your dog. After Sheffield, our first golden, ate a Christmas tree lightbulb and chewed up my wife's glasses, I decided to take out a medical plan on him. It was well worth it!

There are some simple and basic care guidelines to follow, some of which you may be aware of. Dogs need to eat, but not people food. Table scraps, raw meat, raw fish, and cow's milk don't belong in your dog's dish. Even bones can be a problem unless they're pre-boiled, large enough not to be swallowed, and your dog has access for only brief periods of time. Nylon bones are safer because they don't splinter.

Dogs don't groom themselves like cats do, so if you see them chewing or licking a spot, inspect it. When it comes to teeth care, just like you, dogs need to have their teeth brushed and cleaned. When's the last time you had this done for your pup?

Be sure to clean your dog's food and water bowls every day. Everyone is concerned about their dog eating something that is poison, but most people aren't sure what those items might be. Chocolate, oleander bushes, snails that have ingested poison, antifreeze, tobacco products, fruit pits, nail polish, sugar-free gum, are some of the dangerous items. I looked up house, garden, and wild plants, and found more than a hundred that were poisonous to dogs. Look these up in a book or online, and then check your yard and your household to see if anything needs to be removed.

Electrical cords and even the outlets can be fatal temptations.

Everyone assumes dogs can swim and that they love water. That's not true. Many canines have drowned because they were unable to get out of a pool after falling in. One of my dogs fell off a dock once. Fortunately I was there to rescue him.

There are many books that can help you keep your animal safe. Your dog may guard you, and you may guard him.

And what about guarding your own life? We may not face the same threats as our animals, but there are issues we need to be aware of for our safety. Years ago the television-viewing audience was captivated by a police show called *Hill Street Blues*. After their morning briefing and just before the officers hit the streets, the sergeant would say, "Let's be careful out there." He was warning his charges to keep their guard up because the unpredictable could and would happen. That's good advice for us as well.

You and I are faced with issues in the world that entice us to leave behind our Christian standards and values. Scripture warns us again and again to be on guard. Jesus said be on guard against hypocrisy (Matthew 16:6-12), greed (Luke 12:15), persecution (Matthew 10:17), false teaching (Mark 13:22-23), and spiritual slackness and unreadiness for the Lord's return (Mark 13:32-37). "Be careful, or your hearts will be weighed with carousing, drunkenness and the anxieties of life" (Luke 21:34).

Listen to these warnings too. "Be careful that you don't fall" (1 Corinthians 10:12). "Be careful to do what is right" (Romans 12:17). "Be careful that none of you be found to have fallen short" (Hebrews 4:1). "Be careful to do what the LORD your God has commanded you" (Deuteronomy 5:32). "Be careful that you do not forget the LORD" (6:12). "Be careful to obey all that is written in the Book of the Law of Moses" (Joshua 23:6). "Give careful thought to your ways" (Haggai 1:5).

There are reasons for all these warnings! We need to be reminded of temptation areas and from whom we get our strength to resist. If you're struggling with an issue, read these Scripture warnings out loud every morning for a month. Before long you'll know them from memory. That's the best safeguard when temptation starts.[2]

Earthquakes!

Living in Southern California, I grew up experiencing earthquakes and living with the threat of them. Some were large, but many were small. If you want to feel out of control, go through an earthquake! In the early 1950s, I lived through my first major earthquake. It was scary even though the epicenter was more than 100 miles away. Earthquakes are often named after the city closest to it, and this time it was called the Tehachapi earthquake. This one destroyed part of that community as well as a number of the buildings in nearby Bakersfield. I'd been asleep, but the rumblings and shaking sped through the depths of the earth under the hills and woke me and everyone else in the vicinity. My bed shook, and I had to hold on until it subsided. We all got up and said, "What was that?" And then in a louder voice we stated, "Earthquake! And a big one!" The problem with earthquakes is there is little or no warning. It comes from nowhere and throws people off balance, and few people enjoy such disruptive surprises.

Years later I experienced several more major quakes, including one in Whittier, California. That time I was awake—wide awake. I was playing racquetball in an enclosed court. The competition and workout was intense, and all of a sudden I heard what sounded like a freight train. I thought, *Wow, that aerobics class above us is really making a lot of noise.* Then I realized there were no aerobics classes being held above our court. I saw the walls of the court begin to move in and out and realized what was happening. It was an earthquake! The lights went out, and my friend and I ran to the door to escape. We fumbled around to find the door handle, which was recessed into the door so it wasn't easy. Finally we got the door open and raced outside. I found out later the epicenter was only seven miles away. From that day on I never parked in the fitness center's three-level garage for concern that it might crumble in the next earthquake.

I've had friends whose lives were changed by earthquakes. I'll never forget my high school Sunday school teacher sharing about the devastation of his home following the Northridge earthquake. His face reflected the pain of his losses as he described taking a broom and sweeping a path through the debris of more than 60 years of collectables that were shattered as their home came apart.

At least with tornadoes or hurricanes there's some kind of warning. If only we could predict earthquakes. Could dogs help out with this? The idea that animals can sense earthquakes before they occur was first documented in Greece in 373 BC. A number of researchers noted that hours, or in some cases days, before a major earthquake the behavior in dogs changes. Even those who are highly trained begin to pace and act restless and distressed. Their anxiety level intensifies. They bark for no apparent reason, and some run away from home. A geologist in Santa Clara County (California) studied the lost-and-found sections of the newspaper in his area to determine how many cats and dogs were reported missing just prior to an earthquake. There was an increase, and he believes this pattern of animals running away prior to an earthquake has been 80 percent accurate over a 12-year period. This appears to happen with earthquakes of Richter Scale magnitude 3.5 and up.

The predictive ability of dogs has been recognized as being so accurate that in China and Japan, along with high-tech scientific instruments, dogs are considered a necessary part of the national warning system. In 1975, the odd behavior and high anxiety in dogs in Haicheng, a city in China, alarmed officials since they'd observed this behavior in dogs just before earthquakes. Based on this, they ordered the 90,000 residents to evacuate the city. A few hours later, a 7.3 magnitude earthquake struck, destroying 90 percent of the city's buildings. It's estimated that the evacuation, which was based mainly on the animals' responses, saved thousands of lives.

Why do dogs do this? Researchers can only speculate at this time. Many dogs hear high-frequency sounds better than low frequency, so it could be they're hearing some of the pre-tremor sounds. There is much we don't know, but the evidence is clear that dogs do sense when an earthquake is coming.

Earthquakes, tornadoes, and hurricanes create disruption and instability in our physical lives and communities. What about the turbulence and disruption caused in our lives due to everyday occurrences? How can we handle the personal earthquakes that come, often without warning? Scripture gives us valuable insights:

> Peace I leave with you; my peace I give you. I do not give to you as the world gives. Do not let your hearts be troubled and do not be afraid (John 14:27).

> You will guard him and keep him in perfect and constant peace whose mind [both its inclination and its character] is stayed on You, because he commits himself to You, leans on You, and hopes confidently in You (Isaiah 26:3 AMP, brackets in original).

> He will be the stability of your times, a wealth of salvation, wisdom and knowledge; the fear of the LORD is his treasure (Isaiah 33:6 NASB).

Read these verses aloud each day. Let their truths saturate your heart and your mind. They can stabilize you and even prevent some personal earthquakes.[1]

If You Believe This...

Sometimes we need to hear ridiculous stories, especially the kind that bring smiles to our faces or chuckles from deep within. I've found two that I believe are worth passing on. Life can be serious as well as overbearing at times, but even in the midst of grief and sorrow it helps to take a break and experience God's gift called laughter.

A dog story by Will Rogers (1879–1935), America's cowboy humorist, is a rare find. People were more often the butt of his gentle joking. Will Rogers wrote, appeared in movies, and gave lecture tours around the country. He'd swing his lariat 'round in circles and deliver monologues that poked fun at human foibles and made the world laugh when there wasn't always much to laugh at. My brother and I went to his home ranch preserved in Will Rogers State Park, Pacific Palisades, California, several times. It was a bright spot for many people during Will's lifetime. The dog who paid for what he wanted was just one of the characters Rogers met on his travels.

> While I didn't have anything else to do, I got to watching the old spotted dog. He was just an ordinary dog, but when I looked at him close, he was alert and friendly with everyone. Got to inquiring around and found out he'd been bumped off a freight train and seemed to have no owner. He made himself at home and started right in business. When a crowd of cowboys would go into a saloon, he would follow 'em in

and begin entertaining. He could do all kinds of tricks—turn somersaults, lay down and roll over, sit up on his hind feet, and such like.

He would always rush to the door and shake hands with all the newcomers. The boys would lay a coin on his nose, and he'd toss it high in the air and catch it in his mouth and pretend to swallow it. But you could bet your life he didn't swallow it—he stuck it in one side of his lip and when he got a lip full of money, he'd dash out the back door and disappear for a few minutes. What he had really done was hide his money. As soon as he worked one saloon, he would pull out and go to another place.

I got to thinking while watching this old dog, how much smarter he is than me. Here I am out of a job five hundred miles from home and setting around and can't find a thing to do, and this old dog hops off a train and starts right in making money, hand over fist.

Me and some boys around town tried to locate his hidden treasure, but this old dog was too slick for us. He never fooled away time on three or four of us boys that was looking for work. He seemed to know we was broke, but he was very friendly. As he was passing along by me, he'd wag his tail and kinda wink. I musta looked hungry and forlorn. I think he wanted to buy me a meal.

When times was dull and he got hungry, he would mysteriously disappear. Pretty soon he'd show up at a butcher shop with a dime in his mouth and lay it on the counter and the butcher would give him a piece of steak or a bone. He always paid for what he got in the line of grub. Pretty soon he seemed to get tired of the town, and one morning he was gone. A railroad man told us later that he seen the same dog in Trinidad, Colorado.[1]

Veronica Geng has been called "a humorist's humorist." Here is a story she shared, which will probably bring a smile or an amazed expression to your face.

I well remember the days when the Pentagon staffers squirmed as huge expenditures were revealed. $700 toilet seats. $400 hammers. Millions of dollars wasted in unsupervised spending. ([Here's a] document from the Pentagon's ongoing probe into a defense contractor's $87.25 bill for dog boarding.)

Dear Secretary Weinberger:

I have received your request for particulars about the "nauseating" and "preposterous" bill run up at this establishment by Tuffy. I would be more than happy to supply details—I would be *delighted*. As someone who devotes his life to the humane treatment of animals, I welcome this opportunity to enlighten the Department of Defense and the Congress, neither of which seem to have the faintest idea what a dog requires.

Before I get into that, however, may I point out that Canine Chateau is far from being some little fly-by-night dog dorm with a few bunk beds, a Small Business Administration loan, and a penchant for padding its bills to make ends meet. We have been a major and highly profitable concern since 1981.

We are now the largest (and, to my knowledge, the only) kennel in California catering exclusively to the special needs of defense-contractor pets. These animals, as you know, are extremely high-strung and are vulnerable to kidnap by agents of foreign powers who might wish to extort from defense contractors certain classified information (such as details about the offense capability of purported "tie clasps" regularly shipped by the U.S. to El Salvador).

All things considered, then, perhaps I may be forgiven if I preen myself somewhat on our success and our high standards—aesthetic, hygiene, technological *and* finan-cial. Canine Chateau operates under my close personal supervision, and I have something of a reputation among the staff as a strict taskmaster. I wear the key to the pan-try around my neck on a platinum chain; and not only is the level in the kibble bin measured twice a day, but the bin itself is equipped with a state-of-the-art laser lock, which cannot be opened without a micro-coded propyl-ene wafer issued to select personnel only after the most rigorous security check of their backgrounds and habits. Waste of any kind is simply not tolerated—let alone fraud.

Now, as to Tuffy's bill. Tuffy's one-week stay at Canine Chateau was booked under our "No Frills" Plan. We are hardly a dog pound, of course, but I suspect that even you, Secretary Weinberger, with your military barracks frame of reference, would find Tuffy's accommodations Spartan. We have had dogs here—and I'm not going to say *whose* dogs they were, but I think you know the ones I mean— who have run up astronomical bills on shopping sprees at our accessories bar. I'm not criticizing them; most of our dogs are accustomed to a California standard of living, and we can't just suddenly alter a dog's lifestyle because the dog won't understand and will become morose. Nor am I suggesting that you, Secretary Weinberger, would seek favorable publicity at the expense of the innocent animals whose taste for luxuries was created by profits in the very same industries that you depend upon for the perpetuation of your own livelihood and the good of the country. However, I question the Pentagon's decision to

> pay without a peep such previous bills as $3,000 for one golden retriever's ion-drive-propulsion duck decoy with optional remote aerial-guidance system and quartz-fiber splashdown shield, and then to quibble over Tuffy's, which was relatively modest.
>
> But enough. As you requested, I am enclosing an annotated itemization of Tuffy's bill, which I trust will carry my point.[2]

Hopefully you're smiling. Perhaps you're remembering some humorous experiences long forgotten with your own pets. And if someone asks why you have that smile on your face, tell them there are many reasons to smile.

Unfortunately, there are many who smile very rarely. Have you ever smiled after reading a passage of Scripture or hearing a worship song? I have. Sometimes I've caught myself and wondered what I was smiling about. On occasion it's been because of the joy in my heart. The other day I spoke at the memorial service of a good friend. I smiled as I shared and recounted memories even though it was a sad occasion overall.

What brings a smile to your face? As you think about it, consider these passages:

> So I rejoice and am glad. Even my body has hope (Psalm 16:9 NCV).

> Rejoice in the LORD and be glad, you righteous; sing, all you who are upright in heart! (Psalm 32:11).

> Be glad in the Lord and rejoice, you [uncompromisingly] righteous [you who are upright and in right standing with Him]; shout for joy, all you upright in heart! (32:11 AMP, brackets in original).

> "Shout and be glad, Daughter Zion. For I am coming, and I will live among you," declares the LORD (Zechariah 2:10).

Rejoice and be glad, because great is your reward in heaven, for in the same way they persecuted the prophets who were before you (Matthew 5:12).

Perhaps one of the best reasons to smile is reflecting on what God has done for you and how He sees you.

Friendship

Who are your closest friends? Why do you consider them friends? Friends are people you enjoy being with. You delight in their company. You can converse easily, have similar interests, share openly, and depend on them. Your life is more enjoyable and fulfilled when you're with them. There is a mutual, loving trust between you, and you feel safe when you share your needs and thoughts. You believe they will not take advantage of you. These are quality relationships. Patrick Morley, in his book *The Man in the Mirror*, asked some significant questions about friendship:

> Do you have a close friend? I don't just mean someone to call for lunch, but I mean a genuinely *close* friend, a friend like you had in college or high school? The kind of friend you talked to about anything and everything. The kind of friend who just laughed when you said something really dumb. The kind of friend you could really let your hair down with. The kind of friend you knew would be there if you needed someone to talk to, or if you were in real trouble, or if you were hurting.[1]

We all need "stick patient" friends, those who will stick by us when life has gone wrong. Scripture has something to say about friendship too:

Two are better than one, because they have a good return for their labor: If either of them falls down, one can help the other up. But pity anyone who falls and has no one to help them up (Ecclesiastes 4:9-10).

A true friend is always loyal, and a brother is born to help in time of need (Proverbs 17:17 TLB).

One who has unreliable friends soon comes to ruin, but there is a friend who sticks closer than a brother (18:24).

Lots of people flock around a generous person; everyone's a friend to the philanthropist (19:6 MSG).

Wounds from a friend can be trusted, but an enemy multiplies kisses (27:6).

What about your dog as a friend? What have people said about this?

Freud remarked on the fact that "dogs love their friends and bite their enemies, quite unlike people, who are incapable of pure love and always have to mix love and hate in their object relations."[2] In other words, dogs are without the ambivalence with which humans seem cursed. We love, we hate, often the same person, on the same day, maybe even at the same time. This is unthinkable in dogs, whether because, as some people believe, they lack the complexity or, as I believe, they are less confused about what they feel. It is as if once a dog loves you, he loves you always, no matter what you do, no matter what happens, no matter how much time goes by.[3]

Voltaire, who knew about the emotions of dogs, said:

Judge this dog who has lost his master, who has searched for him with mournful cries in every path, who comes home agitated, restless, who runs up and down the stairs, who goes from room to room, who at last finds his beloved master in his study, and shows him his joy by the tenderness of cries, by his leaps, by his caresses."[4]

How many friends respond like this? Sometimes it is even wonderful, as in William James's statement:

> Marvelous as may be the power of my dog to understand my moods, deathless as in his affection and fidelity, his mental state is as unsolved a mystery to me as it was to my remotest ancestor.[5]

Samuel Coleridge, in *Table-Talk* (May 2, 1830), was one of the first to note that

> the best friend a man has in the world may turn against him and become his enemy. His son or daughter…may prove ungrateful. Those who are nearest and dearest to him…may become traitors to their faith…The one absolutely unselfish friend that many can have in this selfish world, the one that never deserts him, the one that never proves ungrateful or treacherous is his dog.[6]

Nobody has written about our response to our "friend" as well as James Thurber:

> Dogs may be Man's best friend, but Man is often Dog's severest critic, in spite of his historic protestations of affection and admiration…He observes, cloudily, that this misfortune or that shouldn't happen to a dog, as if most slings and arrows should, and he describes anybody he can't stand as a dirty dog. He notoriously takes the names of the female dog and her male offspring in vain, to denounce blackly members of his own race. In all this disdain and contempt there is a curious streak of envy, akin to what the psychiatrists know as sibling rivalry. Man is troubled by what might be called the Dog

Wish, a strange and involved compulsion to be as happy and carefree as a dog.[7]

So how are your friendships? Let's take a look using questions from Patrick Morley's *Man in the Mirror*:

Perhaps you have several close friends, or maybe you have none. Or, more likely, you *know* many, but you are not sure just how deep the waters run. Reflect on these questions and see if you have gone far enough to develop some genuine friends.

1. When things go sour and you really feel lousy, do you have a friend you can tell?   Yes   No

2. Do you have a friend you can express any honest thought to without fear of appearing foolish?   Yes   No

3. Do you have a friend who will let you talk through a problem *without* giving you advice? That will be a "sounding board"?   Yes   No

4. Will your friend risk your disapproval to suggest you may be getting off track in your priorities?   Yes   No

5. Do you have a friend who will take the risk to tell you that you are sinning? Or using poor judgment?   Yes   No

6. If you had a moral failure, do you *know* that your friend would stand with you?   Yes   No

7. Is there a friend with whom you feel you are facing life together? A friend to talk over the struggles of life which are unique to you as a man or woman?   Yes   No

8. Do you have a friend you believe you can trust,
   that if you share confidential thoughts they
   will stay confidential?   Yes   No

9. When you are vulnerable and transparent
   with your friend, are you concerned he will
   think less of you?   Yes   No

10. Do you meet with a friend weekly or bi-
    weekly for fellowship and prayer, and
    possibly accountability?   Yes   No[8]

What do your answers say about your friendships?

Do Dogs Worry?

Fear and worry are maladies that are a part of every life. But what about our dogs? Do they have fears? You bet! You've seen it, and so have I. What do you think a little five-pound poodle feels when he's taken to the dog park and immediately sees a large black Lab, a mastiff, and a rottweiler running toward him? That scene could strike fear in the heart of the owner, much less the little dog. Loud, sudden noises create fear in the heart of a dog. Fearful dogs don't always cower. Some may bark and act aggressive.

When my golden retriever Shadow was a few months old, we celebrated the Fourth of July. At twilight, he was romping outside in the backyard. Someone a block away shot off an illegal skyrocket that exploded over our home with an intense sound and brilliant colors. Shadow came running to the house as fast as his legs could move while barking as loud as he could. Needless to say, loud sounds are one of his triggers for barking. Many dogs react to thunderstorms in the same way. Some dogs have constant fears while others exhibit it only occasionally. You can discover what the triggers are if you listen and watch.

We know dogs experience fear, but do they worry like we do? Do they imagine the future like we do? Do they ask, "What if…?" again and again, each time embellishing the possible answers until they're in a state of anxiety? Are their minds and thought processes developed enough that they can cripple themselves emotionally like we sometimes do? When your dog barks at the door of the vet, what's going on in his mind? Is he remembering unpleasant experiences or is he worrying about what the vet is going to do? Is he thinking:

- Oh, no! He neutered me once. What's he going to do this time? There's not much left.

- Every time I come, he sticks a needle in me. It hurts.

- It's really embarrassing. I hate it when he says, "All right, good Fido. Let's take your temperature." I wonder if my owners got their temperature taken that way?

Good questions if you're a dog. So do they worry or not? I'm not sure. If they can't, that's a blessing. There's already enough life to deal with on a daily basis without adding imaginary scenarios. Why are people so prone to worry when we know that it's not good for us?

I have two golden retrievers, Shadow and Aspen. I don't let them have bones to chew on because they're not good for them. But have you ever seen a dog with a bone? We have a phrase for the way a dog handles that treat. He worries it. He gnaws on it day and night. He won't let go, and he may even growl at you if you try to take it away from him. He's looking for meat and the marrow. Dogs will bury bones, then dig them up and gnaw on them again even though the bones are covered with dirt and leaves and who knows what else. He'll bury it and repeat the process again and again.

Our worries are the same. We bite and chew on them. We bury them, dig them up, bury them, and dig them up again. "Worry" comes from the Anglo-Saxon root meaning "to strangle" or "to choke." Worry is the uneasy, suffocating feeling we often experience in times of fear or trouble. When we worry, we're looking pessimistically into the future and thinking of the worst possible outcomes to the situations we're facing. Worry is like a war quietly raging inside. John Haggai describes the conflict this way:

> Worry divides the feelings; therefore the emotions lack stability. Worry divides the understanding; therefore convictions

are shallow and changeable. Worry divides the faculty of perception; therefore observations are faulty and even false. Worry divides the faculty of judging; therefore attitudes and decisions are often unjust. These decisions lead to damage and grief. Worry divides the determinative faculty; therefore plans and purposes, if not "scrapped" altogether, are not filled with persistence.[1]

Gregory Jantz said:

Worry is the ultimate recycler. Any anxiety, fear or concern is reused and recycled endlessly. Worry says if it happened once, it will happen again. Worry says just because it didn't happen doesn't mean it couldn't have. Worry says just because it doesn't happen doesn't mean it won't. Worry says there's no guarantee about tomorrow unless it's a guarantee of disaster. Worry wants to heap up all the actual and perceived disasters of yesterday and pile them on today, as well as any possible problem of tomorrow. This is simply too heavy a load for today to bear; it will crush beneath the weight. Hope gets crushed, joy gets crushed, optimism gets crushed, as does any sense of perspective.

To take charge of your life, you need to start keeping today in line with today. When yesterday is seen through the lens of fear and negativity and tomorrow is viewed as a disaster just waiting to happen, how can anything that happens today be seen as positive? Living in the present gives each day a chance to be viewed as the gift it is.[2]

What can you do with your worries?

Give God your worry in advance (1 Peter 5:7). Peter must have learned from his experience of walking on the water because he later wrote: "Cast all your anxiety on [God] because he cares for you." "Cast" means "to give up" or "to unload." The tense of the verb here refers to a direct, once-and-for-all commitment to God of all anxiety or worry. We're to unload on God our tendency to worry, so that when problems arise we will not worry about them. We can cast our worry on God with confidence because He cares for us.

Center your thoughts on God, not on worry (Isaiah 26:3). Isaiah rejoiced to the Lord, "You will guard him and keep him in perfect and constant peace whose mind [both its inclination and its character] is stayed on You" (AMP, brackets in original). Whatever you choose to think about will either produce or dismiss feelings of anxiety and worry. Those people who suffer from worry are choosing to center their minds on negative thoughts and anticipate the worst. But if your mind or imagination is centered on God—what He has done and will do for you—and the promises of Scripture, peace of mind is inevitable. But *you must choose to center your thoughts in this way.* God has made the provision, but *you must take the action.*

Obedience Classes

Obedience training—that's what they call classes for dog owners. No, they're not really for the dog. Obedience classes may seem to be for the dog, but unless the owners follow the rules of dog training, their dogs will be in control.

There's nothing better than a well-trained, obedient dog, and there's nothing worse than an untrained pooch. Most of the time when our dogs disobey or get into trouble, it's not really their fault—it's ours.

I don't know how many dog owners I've seen who take their dogs to a class for an hour a week and expect their dogs to be trained. They fail to take the 15 to 20 minutes a day required for training and reinforcing the basics. And they wonder why their dogs aren't obedient! It's not their dogs' fault. Like I pointed out before, when my dogs chew up my slippers, are my dogs at fault? No. I'm at fault because I left the slippers accessible, and dogs were born to chew.

Say your Great Dane walks out of the house licking his lips over the pound of butter he just ate that was on the kitchen table. Who left it out and accessible to this gentle giant? Yep, its owner—you. But don't feel bad. All dog owners have made similar mistakes, including me.

One area I used to have trouble with was not returning phone calls. When people called me, I wrote their numbers down on sticky notes and left them by the answering machine so I would return the call later. But in the evening or the next day when I went to call them back, the sticky notes were nowhere to be found. I finally discovered that one of my golden retrievers loved to eat sticky notes! Yes, it was true—my excuse to people was, "My dog ate the note to call you!" However, the solution was simple. Put the notes where my dog couldn't reach them.

Some dogs and some breeds are more difficult to train. Sometimes we wonder, "Will this dog ever get the idea?" Impatience rears its ugly head. I remember trying to teach my first golden to lie down. Day after day I worked, making sure I used an encouraging tone and physically but gently helped him lie down as I repeated the command. For a long time nothing happened when I gave the command by itself. Then one day I walked by and said, "Down!" Sheffield hit the ground and stayed there. I stopped suddenly in shock. *Is this a fluke?* I wondered. Several times that day when I walked by I said, "Down." It worked every time. He'd learned! Why? Because I was consistent and persistent. I obeyed the trainer, and eventually Sheffield obeyed me.

What about you? Do you submit to the dog trainer's teaching and follow through? Does your dog mind what you say? Is your pooch obedient? Does he submit to your requests? Obedience doesn't just happen naturally. You and your dog need to be trained.

I had the good fortune of discovering that one of the best dog trainers in the country lived near me. I signed up for individual lessons for my golden retriever and me. And it really was me getting trained. It was up to me to train my dog, the trainer said. I think my dog enjoyed hearing her tell me what to do and not to do and what to say and what not to say. She was precise, specific, direct (very direct at times), definite, and expected me to respond to the way she did things. And it worked. Why? Because I listened, took it in, wrote down what she said, and then twice a day spent 15 minutes training Shadow and, later, Aspen. Did my dogs always want to obey? No. Did they always obey? Not at first, but eventually they responded positively. And they were so much more enjoyable when they were obedient! I'm sure I was to them as well. They learned to obey and do what I wanted because I obeyed the instructor and did what she thought was best.

Someone once asked me, "Do you think dogs like to obey?" I don't really know because I don't have a dog's mind. But I do know they love to hear "Good dog!" "That a boy!" and "Thank you." I also know they love occasional treats. I'm sure they've learned that being obedient pays off.

Why do dogs disobey? Probably for some of the same reasons we aren't obedient. Why do we ignore the instructions and corrections from others, including God? One reason is stubbornness. Other reasons include insensitivity, indifference, and defensiveness. "I [God] called and you refused, I stretched out my hand and no one paid attention; and you neglected all my counsel and did not want my reproof" (Proverbs 1:24-25 NASB). Sometimes we just openly reject what we're called to do and say, "No, I'll do it my way." We can be stubborn. And sometimes we're dull of hearing. We just don't get it. Basically we say, "I couldn't care less." We give excuses why we don't want to yield. The Hebrew word translated "reproof" means "to be unwilling, unyielding, one who won't consent." Some of us are more this way than others.

Dogs learn it's better to obey than to resist or be stubborn, insensitive, indifferent, or defensive. Perhaps we should learn this from them.

How do you respond to God's request to be obedient? People tend to rationalize their way out of following what they know is best. We cut corners to do things our way. Scripture has so much to say about obedience, including:

> This is what Hezekiah did throughout Judah, doing what was good and right and faithful before the LORD his God. In everything that he undertook in the service of God's temple and in obedience to the law and the commands, he sought his God and worked wholeheartedly. And so he prospered (2 Chronicles 31:20-21).

[Jesus said,] "If you keep my commands, you will remain in my love, just as I have kept my Father's commands and remain in his love" (John 15:10).

Just as through the disobedience of the one man the many were made sinners, so also through the obedience of the one man the many will be made righteous (Romans 5:19).

Because of the service by which you have proved yourselves, others will praise God for the obedience that accompanies your confession of the gospel of Christ, and for your generosity in sharing with them and with everyone else (2 Corinthians 9:13).

We demolish arguments and every pretension that sets itself up against the knowledge of God, and we take captive every thought to make it obedient to Christ (2 Corinthians 10:5).

Peter and the other apostles replied: "We must obey God rather than human beings!" (Acts 5:29).

[To God's elect] who have been chosen according to the foreknowledge of God the Father, through the sanctifying work of the Spirit, to be obedient to Jesus Christ and sprinkled with his blood: Grace and peace be yours in abundance (1 Peter 1:2).

Being found in appearance as a man, [Jesus] humbled himself by becoming obedient to death—even death on a cross! (Philippians 2:8).

Dancing Dogs

I thought I was the only one who enjoyed watching dancing dogs. Yes, dancing dogs. I've seen them on TV. I even purchased a DVD of a choreographed dance between an owner and her golden retriever. They danced to the music from *Grease*. When I see something unique like that, one of my first responses is, "How did they train their dogs to do that?" After watching this video, I investigated. I found a series of training DVDs on how to teach dogs to dance. And yes, I bought them. It's not as hard as you might suppose, but then I haven't gone any further than watching the videos. For one thing, I don't have that much free time on my hands to train my dogs to dance. Another reason is that I'm a terrible dancer. I'd hate to have my dogs show me up!

I found an interesting story about dancing dogs in the book *Paws for Reflection*. One of the authors shared this:

> My dogs dance. It's a trick I taught them. Biscuit rises high on her hind legs and twirls. Morgan used to perform a more wobbly turn, but now that he's older and has some back problems he "dances" by walking in a circle. Becca spins rapidly on the ground and sometimes lifts her front paws as she does so. Though my dogs' styles vary, they all dance for the very same reason. They want the tasty treat they know it will earn them. That is good enough motivation that sometimes they'll even initiate dancing on their own to see if they can trigger a treat when they choose.

Lately I've been watching some dance competitions on television. These contests also offer rewards. On one show, couples compete for a large trophy and bragging rights. On another, dancers vie for a huge cash prize. Even those who don't win the top "treat" get other rewards, such as new friendships and the new steps and experiences they've encountered that might help improve their lives and careers. All of those are good reasons to dance.

None of them are Jessica's.

Jessica is my favorite dancer. She isn't on those dancing shows. She isn't even on her feet. Jessica is 12, and she's afflicted with cerebral palsy. She dances in her wheelchair.

I met Jessica through her mother. She specializes in plant care, and she's worked for my family for years. Recently she showed me a DVD of Jessica dancing with her teacher. The young girl was a beautiful portrait of joy in motion. Jessica danced with her arms and wheelchair gracefully moving in time to the music as she propelled herself across the floor and in circles. Jessica's teacher twirled her arms and body in a fluid duet with her pupil.

I've seen some marvelous choreography on those dance shows, but this touched my heart so much more. Jessica's dance made my heart leap at the endless possibilities of an indomitable spirit. It proved creative expression can soar despite life's challenges. I was reminded that we all have the potential to create because we've been made in the image of our great Creator God.[1]

The Scriptures talk about dancing:

Let Israel rejoice in their Maker, let the people of Zion be glad in their King. Let them praise his name with dancing and make music to him with timbrel and harp. For the LORD takes delight in his people; he crowns the humble with victory. Let his faithful people rejoice in this honor and sing for joy on their beds (Psalm 149:2-5).

One of my favorite authors, Ken Gire, has written the most inspiring devotional books I've ever read (and reread). One of them uses dance to describe our relationship with our Savior. It's called *The Divine Embrace—An Invitation to the Dance of Intimacy with Christ*. He begins this book by describing an encounter he had with the "Emperor's Waltz" and shares his thoughts about the emperor being our Lord Jesus. He then gives this description of our Lord dancing with us:

> Maybe it's not so much lessons in dancing we need as lessons in loving, because the Christian life is about intimacy, not technique. The Lord of the dance doesn't want us worrying about our feet. He doesn't want us wondering about the steps ahead. He merely wants us to feel the music, fall into his arms, and follow his lead.
>
> There are places he wants to take us on the dance floor, things he wants to show us, feelings he wants to share with us, words he wants to whisper in our ear. This is what the divine embrace is—an invitation to a more intimate relationship with Christ, one exhilarating, ennobling, uncertain step at a time.
>
> We have a choice, you and I. And it's a choice we make every day, throughout the day. The choice is this:
>
> > We can dance.
> > Or we can sit it out.
>
> If we dance, we may step on his toes. And he may step on ours. We may stumble and bump into other people. We may fall on our faces and make fools of ourselves. People may talk, they may avoid us, they may even ridicule us.
>
> If you fear those things, you may want to sit it out.
>
> If you do, you won't have to worry. You'll be safe in your seat along the wall.
>
> You'll also miss the dance.
>
> More importantly, you'll miss the romance.
>
> At some time or another, I have chosen to sit it out. Fear

was a big reason. Fear of the attention it would bring—and perhaps the criticism. Fear of embarrassment and possible estrangement. Fear of not being in control of my life, my career, my future. Fear of being led to places that would be uncomfortable, even painful.

There are two things I have learned from the divine embrace.

That perfect love really does cast out fear.

And that I would rather dance poorly with Jesus than sit perfectly with anyone else.[2]

Favorite Dog Stories

If you're a dog lover, you know many stories—dog stories that is. You've read them, you've watched them, you've experienced them. One of the numerous and retained images I have came about when I was six and watched *Lassie Come Home*. This was the story of a faithful collie who travels a thousand miles from Northern Scotland to England to return to the boy she loves. Lassie climbed mountains, swam rivers, fought with other dogs, and did whatever it took to get home. I remember going home after the show and telling one of my parents about the movie. I kept crying because of some of the sad scenes in the film.

Do you remember other classic dog tales? *Old Yeller, Lady and the Tramp, Lad—A Dog, 101 Dalmations, Greyfriars Bobby, Homeward Bound, Marley and Me,* and *Beethoven*? A classic tale is Jack London's *Call of the Wild*. The story takes place in the Gold Rush days in the Klondike (Alaska). A man named Thornton has a sled dog named Buck, and the two care deeply for one another:

> [Thornton] had a way of taking Buck's head roughly between his hands, and resting his own head upon Buck's, of shaking him back and forth, the while calling him ill names that to Buck were love names. Buck knew no greater joy than that rough embrace and the sound of murmured oaths, and at

each jerk back and forth it seemed that his heart would be shaken out of his body so great was its ecstasy...

Buck had a trick of love expression that was akin to hurt. He would often seize Thornton's hand in his mouth and close so fiercely that the flesh bore the impress of his teeth for some time afterward. And as Buck understood the oaths to be love words, so the man understood this feigned bite for a caress.

For the most part, however, Buck's love was expressed in adoration. While he went wild with happiness when Thornton touched him or spoke to him, he did not seek these tokens... He would lie by the hour, eager, alert, at Thornton's feet, looking up into his face, dwelling upon it, studying it, following with keenest interest each fleeting expression, every movement or change of feature.[1]

One day in a gold camp full of prospectors, some men were bragging about the ability of their sled dogs. One thing lead to another, and Thornton bet a thousand dollars worth of gold dust that Buck could pull a thousand pounds of gear on a sled for one hundred yards. Now Buck had never achieved this feat. After his bet was accepted, Thornton was troubled. Buck was strong, but Thornton wasn't sure if he could do it. Plus the sled's skids had frozen into place, so Buck would have to break the ice too. Thornton loved Buck and didn't want him to hurt himself. He didn't want to go through with the bet, but because of the pressure of others he didn't back down. Amid the excitement of the bet and attempt, Thornton kneeled down in front of Buck:

He took [Buck's] head in his two hands and rested cheek to cheek...He whispered in his ear, "As you love me, Buck. As you love me," was what he whispered. Buck whined with suppressed eagerness.[2]

Perhaps this phrase we have all thought or said or wanted to express because there is such love between us and our dogs. And the outcome of the test? Buck puts forth a tremendous effort and pulls the sled the full distance. In the midst of the victory celebration, Thornton falls to his knees in front of Buck and weeps openly. Then came a playful yet meaningful moment between the two: "Buck seized Thornton's hand in his teeth. Thornton shook him back and forth.[3]

I understand this connection. I hope you do too. We know what it means. I remember many vivid scenes from *The Call of the Wild*—the book and the film. These many years later I can still bring up images of people struggling under water and trying to hang onto their gold after the ice broke. I also remember the loyalty and devotion of Buck.

Dogs remind us of how to love others. Does that seem a bit odd to you? Dogs, like other animals, didn't just happen. They are a purposeful creation by God. You and I have been the recipients of many gifts in life (although some we may not see as gifts). Our dogs are gifts to us—gifts designed to make us feel valued and special. I know my dogs care about me. They want to be with me. Is it love? I believe it is. If they could, they would be by my side all the time. Dogs don't talk like we do, of course. They can't say, "I'm devoted to you. I care for you. I love you." But like Buck showed how much he loved Thornton, your dog shows you how much you're loved.

There is one other being who loves us so much it's beyond our comprehension. Have you ever repeated aloud again and again "God loves me!"? Try it some time. Let the words and meaning override everything else that is going on in your life. I believe you'll find it will make a huge difference! Memorize John 3:16 and repeat it often:

> God so loved the world that he gave his one and only Son, that whoever believes in him shall not perish but have eternal life (John 3:16).

Many people have expressed how much Dick Dickinson's paraphrase of 1 Corinthians 13:4-8 has helped them. I recommend you read it out loud every morning for a week or a month and see how your concept of God, His responses to you, and your acceptance of Him will change. This is a wonderful description of God's love!

Because God loves me, He is slow to lose patience with me.

Because God loves me, He takes the circumstances of my life and uses them in a constructive way for my growth.

Because God loves me, He does not treat me as an object to be possessed and manipulated.

Because God loves me, He has no need to impress me with how great and powerful He is because *He is God*, nor does He belittle me as His child in order to show me how important He is.

Because God loves me, He is for me. He wants to see me mature and develop in His love.

Because God loves me, He does not send down His wrath on every little mistake I make, of which there are many.

Because God loves me, He does not keep score of all my sins and then beat me over the head with them whenever He gets a chance.

Because God loves me, He is deeply grieved when I do not walk in the ways that please Him because He sees this as evidence that I don't trust Him and love Him as I should.

Because God loves me, He rejoices when I experience His power and strength and stand up under the pressures of life for His name's sake.

Because God loves me, He keeps on working patiently with me even when I feel like giving up and can't see why He doesn't give up on me too.

Because God loves me, He keeps on trusting me at times when I don't even trust myself.

Because God loves me, He never says there is no hope for me; rather, He patiently works with me, loves me, and disciplines me in such a way that it is hard for me to understand the depth of His concern for me.

Because God loves me, He never forsakes me even though many of my friends might.

Because God loves me, He stands with me when I have reached the rock bottom of despair, when I see the real me and compare that with His righteousness, holiness, beauty and love. It is at a moment like this that I can really believe that God loves me.

Yes, the greatest of all gifts is God's perfect love![4]

Political Dogs

Imagine a canine convention that took place when the United States was being established. Picture every breed imaginable coming together. They elect a leader, who chooses his cabinet. After days of deliberation with his advisors, the lead dog calls the hundreds of dogs together:

> Our chance has come! This is our opportunity to influence the independence, growth, and direction of this new nation. "How can we do that because we're only dogs?" Easy, my friends. We'll become presidential dogs…and many of our offspring will do the same. We will be loved, cared for, pampered—and become influencers without the politicians realizing what we're doing! It's a great plan!

Did you visualize the scene? And perhaps it was carried out because 25 of the 44 presidents the United States has had so far have owned dogs—and usually more than one. George Washington set the tone by owning 30 hounds, including one by the name of Sweet Lips! Washington is credited with creating the foxhound breed.

Some of the presidents might be considered hoarders. Presidents Herbert Hoover and John Kennedy each had 9 dogs. President Calvin Coolidge owned 12! Can you imagine the feeding and cleanup that took place everywhere the presidents and their dogs went? (I hope this wasn't a task the Secret Service got stuck with.)

There are many interesting facts, stories, and events that involve the presidential dogs. Here are a few to pique your interest.

- Thomas Jefferson was a dog lover and instituted the first dog license.

- Theodore Roosevelt's bull terrier named Pete almost created an international incident when he bit at and ripped the French ambassador's pants.

- Warren Harding's dog, Laddie Boy, had his own chair at cabinet meetings.

- Ronald Reagan was photographed with his dog Lucky and British Prime Minister Margaret Thatcher. Lucky was pulling the president across the White House lawn.

- One of Franklin Roosevelt's terriers, Falon, became a star in an MGM Hollywood movie about a "typical day of a dog in the White House."

- Richard Nixon's black-and-white cocker spaniel named Checkers became famous when Nixon refused to give him up because he was a gift. The now-famous "Checker's Speech" improved Nixon's political fortunes.

- George Bush Sr.'s dog Millie gave birth while in the White House. Millie was the first presidential dog to "write" a book. *Millie's Book* rose to #1 on the *New York Times* bestsellers list.

- President Reagan's Bavarian des Flander dog, Lucky, chased newsmen around the White House and attended strategy sessions in the Oval Office.

- John Kennedy's dog, Pushinka, was a gift from Soviet Premier Nikita Khrushchev. Pushinka, a mongrel, was born to Srieka, a Soviet space dog. Eventually, Pushinka and Charlie, a Welsh terrier, produced four puppies that Kennedy affectionately called pupniks.

- When President Obama and his family were looking for a dog, they chose a Portuguese water dog named Bo.

One of the best anecdotes about President Ford and his Irish setter Liberty happened when the kennel keeper was off duty. The president happily took Liberty for an evening walk. That night, just like every night, the presidential quarters of the White House was secured. Unfortunately for President Ford, he didn't inform the Secret Service he was taking Liberty for a walk, so the president and Liberty got locked out! Ford had to get security to let him back in.

I doubt whether most presidents are in charge of feeding, watering, and training their dogs. Their dogs are in the limelight, yes. They get a lot of press. Although no newsperson follows your dog around, your pup probably receives plenty of one-on-one care and attention from you. Even if he isn't famous, your dog is special to you. And that's what counts.

Isn't it great to feel special? I hope you know your dog is special—and so are you! I know there are days when you don't feel special. Regardless, you are! Jesus said a lot about who you are. He said you're the salt of the earth. You're the light of the world. So when you're wondering where you fit in, wondering if anyone cares about you, or wondering if you're making a difference, don't look to the people around you for answers or satisfaction. Look to the One who really cares about you—your heavenly Father! His Word will remind you that you count, that you are loved, that you are part of the family of the King of the universe, Jesus Christ. Read these Scriptures out loud every morning and evening. Let them serve as a reminder of who you are in God's eyes:

> Do not worry about your life, what you will eat or drink; or about your body, what you will wear. Is not life more than food, and the body more than clothes? Look at the birds of the air; they do not sow or reap or store away in barns, and yet your heavenly Father feeds them. *Are you not much more valuable than they?* (Matthew 6:25-26).

Cast all your anxiety on [God] because he cares for you (1 Peter 5:7).

You [Lord] created my inmost being; you knit me together in my mother's womb (Psalm 139:13).

I [the Lord] have engraved you on the palms of my hands; your walls are ever before me (Isaiah 49:16).

[Our Lord Jesus Christ] chose us in him before the creation of the world to be holy and blameless in his sight (Ephesians 1:4).

[Jesus said,] "Do not rejoice that the spirits submit to you, but rejoice that your names are written in heaven" (Luke 10:20).

Remember:

- You are more *valuable* than any animal.
- God *cares* for you.
- You were *created* by God.
- You are *engraved* upon the hand of God.
- You are *chosen* by Him.
- Your name is *written* in heaven.
- You can have a wonderful day by remembering how special you are to your Lord and Savior Jesus Christ.

Growing Older

An older dog walked by my house the other day. Her name is Sandy. She had a rough life for a couple of years. Her former owners didn't want her, so they didn't take very good care of her. A golden retriever rescue group stepped in and brought her to a safer place. She needed some teeth removed, and even though she was older and her coat was unkempt, a couple loved her and adopted her.

Now Sandy is twelve. She walks slowly but still wags her tail. She's not very alert, but she still enjoys her surroundings. She doesn't run after a ball now, but she still trots after it. Her muscles aren't as strong as they used to be, but she still gets around. She's pretty much reached the life expectancy for that breed. She sleeps more than she used to. When I talk to her, her tail still wags back and forth. After I saw her the other day, I wondered, *Do dogs think about getting older? Do they know their time is limited? Do they think about death? Do they realize their bodies aren't going to get stronger? What about their memory? Is it as sharp as it was?*

Aging…have you given it any thought? Maybe you're not there yet, but maybe you are. As I write these words, I'm approaching my seventy-fifth birthday. Someone said just the other day, "Gee, Norm, you'll be three-quarters of a century old." *Oh great,* I thought. *That puts a different slant on it.* But I'm thankful for this year, and I'm thankful for each day of life God gives me. Life is a gift.

Yes, we're impacted by aging. Our minds may operate more slowly, and our short-term memories may not be as sharp. But most aspects of intelligence and memory stay intact, so we can change directions or adjust to slowing down and coping with the ravages of time and disease. What we do to stretch and exercise our brains makes a difference. Creativity doesn't necessarily decrease with age. Many people do their best work during their older years. All those years of experience and accumulated wisdom count for something. The attitude factor also makes a huge difference.[1]

The Bible offers a positive heritage model. It says old age is a blessing, a gift from God to be valued by the entire community. As believers, our calling is not to treat aging as a disease to be prevented, treated, or cured. God, the Giver of Life, doesn't indicate how long we'll live or assure us that following Him and His guidance guarantees longevity. The more important question isn't how long we live but *how* we live.

Do you accept your age? Are you adjusting to the various changes in your life? How do you face the fact that you'll be older and different in 10 years? Paul Tournier said,

> It is no easy matter to accept that one is growing old, and no one succeeds in doing it without first overcoming his spontaneous refusal. It is difficult, too, to accept the growing old of someone else, of one's nearest and dearest. The aging of a father whose judgment and advice always used to seem so sound, but whom one can no longer consult because he must not be worried, or because his faculties are failing. The aging of a friend to whom one no longer talks as one used to, because it is necessary to shout out loud things that used to be said quite quietly. It is hard to accept the decay of conversation into banality, empty optimism and insignificance.[2]

True, we used to do some things we can no longer do, and we do things now we'll no longer be able to do a few years from now. Here's the thing: We'll live differently, but we won't live less. Despite limitations, let's not overlook what we *can* do. Let's not fail to ask God to direct and guide us now and in the future. Yes, there will be one!

> "I know the plans I have for you," declares the LORD, "plans to prosper you and not to harm you, plans to give you hope and a future" (Jeremiah 29:11).

> Call to me and I will answer you and tell you great and unsearchable things you do not know (33:3).

We can approach growing older in several ways. One is grasping the past and holding on tightly. Another response is withdrawing into apathy about life. A third approach is choosing to live life fully, whatever it will entail. This is being present and active. Ambition is still present but has been redirected to accommodate this new life phase. You may discover a new purpose and set new goals. There is new *meaning* based on how you're living to further God's kingdom. Paul Tournier writes about this time of life:

> Living with Jesus means living every detail of my daily life in that light. It does not mean detaching myself from the world and from the immediate concerns which give meaning to my life. I do not have to deny or oppose these provisional meanings of my life, but I shall be able to distinguish the transcendent meaning in every provisional meaning. Where is God leading me in these daily events?[3]

Growing older means detaching from the past, and it means attaching to the present and the future. It's choosing life now and choosing a future that will last for eternity.

Tsunami Dog

The world is full of disasters. We experience earthquakes, tornadoes, hurricanes, and tsunamis, just to name a few. Some come from the hands of people, such as the bombing in Oklahoma City (1995) or the terrorist attack on United States soil September 11, 2001, while others are the result of nature running amok. I was a counselor who helped the traumatized people after the attack in New York (9/11), and I've counseled victims of some of the mass shootings the United States has experienced lately. I've seen the evil mankind can create. I've also seen the devastation in the aftermath of terrible storms, including Katrina, so I know what nature can cause. These types of experiences leave an imprint on us that lasts for years and years. Usually the stories that make the news following such disasters are filled with death and destruction. Now and then there may be one or two that brings hope to the heart and smiles to our faces. That's the case with "Tsunami Dog."

In 2004, a tsunami hit Thailand (caused by a 9.1 magnitude earthquake, the second largest ever recorded. It lasted 8 to 10 minutes. More than 230,000 lives were lost in 14 countries). The Associated Press editors were weary of all the tragic stories and requested some positive news. People needed some good news after all the devastation and loss. One reporter found some news regarding a scruffy yellow dog by the name of Selnakumar.

In a small coastal fishing village of Chinnakalajset, India, 20 percent of the population were killed by the waves. This skinny dog belonged to a fisherman who had three sons, ages three, five, and seven. The dog was very close to the oldest boy, Dinakaran, and they'd been together five years. In this poor village there was barely enough food for the family, so the dog was on his own. Leftover fishing scraps and an occasional rat made up his diet.

Fishermen in India belong to a "low caste." They're generally separated from society, and in this area they lived in ramshackle huts near the beach. Beyond the village was a high hill that had to be climbed to get to the highway. Up there is also where the wealthy people lived.

The day the tsunami hit, the family heard a strange sound. People were yelling and screaming. The father and mother climbed on the roof to see better and were shocked by the view unfolding in front of them. The ocean had receded, leaving the sand bare. Fish were stranded all over the sand, and people from the village were running around and gathering up as many of them as possible. But then Dinakaran's father saw a sight that struck fear in his heart. A gigantic wave, not too far out, was rapidly making its way to shore. Dinakaran's father yelled, "Run, run!" to his family.

Terror and chaos reigned. Panic was an understatement. Those who hadn't run for years were straining every muscle to climb the hill to sanctuary and safety. Some parents were dragging their children, while others were more concerned for their own lives. Even animals were running. Those who looked back at the massive wave tended to become immobilized by the sight of the impending disaster.

Dinakaran's mother picked up their three-year-old and five-year-old. As she ran for the hill, she called for Dinakaran to follow them. But he didn't. In a panic, he ran for the safest place a seven-year-old knows—the house. He quickly slid under his bed.

In the confusion going up the hill, Dinakaran's parents assumed their eldest son had followed and was safe. But he hadn't, and he wasn't.

In the hut, Dinakaran was under the bed but he wasn't alone. His dog had followed him, but he wasn't calm. The dog nipped at the boy and bit into his clothing. He tried to drag the boy from under the bed to get him to leave the house. Finally the dog grabbed the boy's collar and pulled. Dinakaran got up, and then the dog began herding him like a sheep. He nipped at his master's heels until the boy was running up the hill with the stragglers from the village.

The wave hit, and Dinakaran's parents searched frantically for their boy. When they found him, they were overjoyed. They listened in amazement to the story of how the yellow dog had persisted until Dinakaran had run up the hill. The dog's master had strayed from the herd, so the dog went after him and brought him back.

The news correspondent who heard this story was skeptical at first, but after checking with eyewitnesses, he knew the tale was true. This story appeared in just about every newspaper in the world and was translated into many languages. A skinny, yellow, nondescript dog in a small fishing village in India created good news amid the terrible destruction of the 2004 tsunami.[1]

Someone else has created even more amazing news. Similar to this yellow dog's seeking out his master to bring him to safety, God sought out every person in the entire world and offered him and her safety and eternal life if each person would accept His Son, Jesus Christ, as personal Lord and Savior. As Dinakarin's mother wept tears of joy when he was found, and as a shepherd rejoices when he finds a lost sheep, God too is delighted when we turn to Him and accept His offer of love, redemption, mercy, and grace.

The villagers found their physical safety at the top of a hill. Another hill provides soul safety along with eternal salvation for everyone who chooses to believe in God and His Son, Jesus—it's called Calvary.

How Do You Love?

Do you love your dog? I'm sure you do. Does your dog love you? Probably more than you realize. We humans believe we know how to love, but do we really? Not in a pure way. Often our love is distorted, or it's a mixture of love and distortion, or sometimes it's even conditional. Our love is seldom pure because there is so much that can get in the way. For instance, our brains interfere with how we love. Our thought lives can block love's flow. David Teems, in his book *And Thereby Hangs a Tale*, describes this well:

> Distractions [from love] come in many forms. *Thinking* is one of them. The mind of man possesses boundless capacity, but as busy as it is, as great a machine as it has proven to be, with as much swiftness and precision as the wheels can spin, it can be its worst enemy in matters of the heart.
>
> Thinking is perhaps the greatest impediment to love. Love and logic are incompatible. We cannot talk ourselves into love nor can we reason it away. Reason only interferes. Love engages completely different parts of us, an altogether different precinct, the one closer to divinity, closer to our origins.
>
> There was a time when heart and mind were at peace with the other, when they lived in absolute agreement, in a time when the heart had preeminence over mind, when man understood his own heart, when there was no distance

between him and his origins, when the heart held the seat of power. The mind of man was free to operate at full capacity because it was under dominion. Love was sovereign. The heart was not yet a thing to be redeemed.[1]

Our memories and our past get in the way. Think about your dog. Is he distracted from loving by memories? Hardly. Think about this:

A dog's memory is still better than a human's. Some may argue this point. But if it is true, perhaps it is because you and I overburden our memories with emotional millstones. The processing is what makes the difference. Whatever the truth, a dog has the capability to engage fully in the moment, to give the moment all her attention. She is willing to invest all of herself to the moment because the moment is all that exists for her.

Because she pays no homage to time, the dog can draw from life its fullest measures, its boundless liberality and generosity, the things we deny ourselves. When she plays, she plays hard and completely. When she loves, she invests her entire being. In grief she holds back nothing. In her possession of the moment, the dog maintains a certain preparation for whatever happens, a readiness that tenders time and its odd hypnosis mute.

For memory to work properly, there has to be some perception of time somewhere, some observance of its rule. Dogs will delight in people or animals they have known or have come to love even when separated by long stretches of time. In Homer's classic tale *The Odyssey,* Odysseus has been away from home for 20 years. On his return, his dog, Argos, now old, feeble, immobile, lying on a dung heap, full of fleas, uncared for but still alive, upon hearing his master's voice, recognizes him immediately. The dog doesn't have the strength to move toward him, but he wags his tail and lowers his ears in pure joy. Odysseus has to wipe a tear from his own face lest his identity be detected. The dog then dies fulfilled and happy. (Between you and me, I suspect Homer had a dog.)

For the dog, a past is expedient only as it helps trigger alarm or delight.

You and I have a more complicated relationship with time than the dog does. Dogs do not burden themselves with souvenirs, emotional or otherwise. This may explain their exceptional ability to forgive.

Dogs actually live like there is no tomorrow. Life is reduced to a succession of clearly definable moments. This clarifies love for them and simplifies their faith. It defines the way they are able to love us. "I will give all to you *now* because *now* is what I have. *Now* is all I understand. *Now* has shaped my thought life and taught me how to love you."[2]

Jack London, in his book *White Fang*, describes the love of a dog. The following account beautifully describes the transformation of a dog overcome with love for his master:

White Fang was in the process of finding himself. In spite of the maturity of his years and of the savage rigidity of the mould that had formed him, his nature was undergoing an expansion…His old code of conduct was changing.

Like had been replaced by love. And love was the plummet dropped down into the deeps of him where like had never gone. And responsive out of his deeps had come the new thing—love. That which was given unto him did he return. This was a god indeed, a love-god, a warm and radiant god, in whose light White Fang's nature expanded as a flower expands under the sun…

His love partook of the nature of worship, dumb, inarticulate, a silent adoration. Only by the steady regard of his eyes did he express his love, and by the unceasing following with his eyes of his god's every movement. Also, at times, when his god looked at him and spoke to him, he betrayed an awkward self-consciousness, caused by the struggle of his love to express itself and his physical inability to express it.[3]

Dogs don't merely play at love. They actually mean it. That is why it is such a lovely spectacle of nature. Shakespeare wrote, "A dog is utterly sincere. It cannot pretend."[4] Perhaps that is the real reason we enjoy them so much, simply because their thought life isn't quite the tangle ours seem to be. They demand nothing from us but us.

"Dogs do not lie to you about how they feel because they cannot lie about feelings."[5] We try to make a kind of happiness:

Devotion is not a game to the dog. She takes it seriously. She is vigilant. She seems to know how it works and why it is important. Devotion is visceral. It defines her. It makes the awe of nature visible, almost audible, telling quite profoundly of a Creator that stashes bits of himself in all he creates and who defines himself by one thing—love. Every action he takes has that one life behind it. It is the single motive in his heart.

The dog also sets no limits on who is worthy of her love. Forgive my presumption, but the dog exercises a radical Christianity that observes no reference whatsoever. Her love is not colored with bias or preferment. Her love has no politics. It knows neither rank nor station. She can love at either end of the social horizon with just as much veracity and fearlessness, just as much joy and bubble. Beggar, prince, new money, old money, no money, it matters as little to the dog as it does to God.

This brings us back to the dog. *Joyful, joyful, joyful!* In all creation below man there is no more intense lover than the dog, and there is perhaps no creature happier. She is sold out. Devotion *is* life to her. She has rediscovered her paradise.

And she knows her redeemer. She studies him. She aches

in the absence of him. Sometimes she aches in his presence. Without worship even the dog knows life is missing something necessary, something written on nature itself.[6]

Without worship something is missing in our lives too.

So what have you learned about love from your dog? Better yet what have you learned about love from God?

Love is patient, love is kind. It does not envy, it does not boast, it is not proud. It does not dishonor others, it is not self-seeking, it is not easily angered, it keeps no record of wrongs. Love does not delight in evil but rejoices with the truth. It always protects, always trusts, always hopes, always perseveres (1 Corinthians 13:4-7).

We are able to love because God first loved us. Perhaps dogs can help us understand love better and express it more.

What Do You Do?

Bring a group of people together, and in time the conversation will probably get around to this question: "What do you do?" We talk about our work, our jobs, our purpose in life. Can you imagine bringing a group of dogs together and listening to their chatter? What would they talk about? Perhaps the conversation would go something like this.

"So what do you guys do?"

"I herd for a living. It's bred into me, and I love it."

"I'm a flusher," one spaniel stated.

"I point for a living."

"I'm a terrorist."

"I'm a toy, and I'm cute!"

Dogs were bred for a purpose. The breeds all have similarities and differences. Regardless of the dog you have, they all came from the same source—wolves. Yep, your dog's ancestor thousands of years ago was a wolf. The wolf was one of the first animals to be tamed, and the tamed wolf's job was being a hunting companion. From those wolves we now have around 400 dog breeds.

Because of selective breeding controlled by people, we have dogs who love to swim and those who can't stand to get their paws wet.

Some were bred specifically to be watchdogs, such as rottweilers and German shepherds, and some were bred primarily for hunting, such as retrievers and spaniels.

Classifying dogs is not an exact science, but generally speaking dogs fall into seven broad categories. Can you name them? Here they are: hounds, sporting dogs, herding dogs, terriers, working dogs, non-sporting dogs, and toys. Which category does your dog fall into?

Let's take a look at the "selective seven."

Hounds have been crucial in hunting and tracking. Scent hounds were bred to follow odor trails. They usually have short legs to help keep their noses close to the ground. Their big, flopping ears are like fans that help direct the odors into their faces. Sight hounds have great eyesight and can spot their quarries from great distances. Hounds, like people, sometimes get so involved in their quest they don't hear commands when on the hunt.

What's a *sporting dog*? They're also known as gun dogs, and their primary purpose is to retrieve any game that's been shot. Let's add to our knowledge (this could be overload). The category of "sporting dog" has four separate groups: setters, pointers, retrievers, and spaniels. Setters do just that, they sit and stare at where the game is. Pointers run close to where the game is and point, using the classic pose of one front leg folded back, nose straight toward the prey, and tail extended straight. Retrievers flush game and retrieve any that have been brought down. Their coats are generally water repellent. Spaniels are used for flushing game and also retrieving game that has been brought down, whether on land or in water.

I took Sheffield, my first golden retriever, pheasant hunting one day. I didn't have to teach him anything. He searched for a bird in the classic back-and-forth pattern, and when it flew up I shot it. Sheffield then found the dead bird, picked it up gently, and brought it back. His pride was evident. "I did it!" his attitude said. Another time a friend and I were hunting in Nebraska with a black lab who had way too much energy. He ran ahead of us, flushing everything in sight so fast that we didn't have time to get off a lot of shots. The next day we let him out of the truck a mile from where we planned to hunt. He ran off all his excess energy, and once at the hunting field he flushed and retrieved perfectly. Retrievers and spaniels are the movers and shakers of the sporting dogs category. They usually love to get wet and enjoy swimming. Most sporting dogs require regular, invigorating exercise. Here is a brief listing of sporting dogs:

Setters: English setter, Gordon setter, Irish setter, Irish red-and-white setter, Picardy setter

Pointers: Bracco Italiana (Italian pointer), Brittany spaniel, English pointer, German shorthaired pointers, German wirehaired pointers, Hungarian vizsla, Portuguese pointers, Spanish pointers, Weimaraner wirehaired pointing griffons

Retrievers: Chesapeake Bay retriever, flat-coated retriever, golden retriever, Labrador retriever, Nederlandse kooikerhondje, Nova Scotia duck tolling retriever

Flushing dogs: American water spaniel, cocker spaniel, clumber spaniel, English cocker spaniel, English springer spaniel, field spaniel, Sussex spaniel, Welsh springer spaniel[1]

Sporting breeds make ideal pets because they're highly trainable. They've been bred to obey and are eager to serve.

Herding dogs were developed thousands of years ago in Asia by nomadic shepherds. The dogs work in groups or individually. These dogs need an abundance of physical and mental exercise. They will herd geese, sheep, cattle, and yes, even children!

Terriers can be feisty. Some even call them miniature terrorists. They were developed to kill vermin, such as rats, and dig out small prey. They're full of energy and entertaining, but they can be temperamental.

Working dogs really work. They pulled carts, turned water wheels, agitated butter churns, and were hooked up to turn spits for cooking.

Non-sporting dogs are bred for unique purposes. Some became guard dogs for royalty. Bulldogs were bred to help bring down wild bulls. They were trained to attack and grab, holding on to the animal no matter what! Many of these breeds are born with such massive jaws and heads they sometimes have to be delivered by caesarean section.

The toy category isn't really full of toys, of course. They're real dogs, small in stature but often large in personality. These pups love to be spoiled. They were bred to be companions so they enjoy being close to people.[2]

There is one more category: *mixed breeds*, otherwise known as mixed, mutts, and mongrels. These dogs are just as significant as the purebred ones. Some mixed breeds eventually end up as "designer breeds," such as the American labradoodle (Labrador and poodle mix) and the cockapoo (cocker spaniel and poodle mix).

Each category, as well as each breed, has its own characteristics as well as purpose. Sometimes we call these gifts. We as "dog servants," which is more true than calling ourselves dog owners, have a variety of unique gifts as well. We need all the various abilities of the various dogs, just as we need the various abilities of the people in our lives. In the body of Christ, also known as "the church," we have a mixture of people with different personalities, abilities, and spiritual gifts, which provides a rich texture and multitude of strengths to draw on to meet the needs of the members and reach out to others.

There are different kinds of gifts in the church, but the same Holy Spirit distributes them. There are different kinds of service, but they all are geared to serve Jesus Christ. There are different kinds of working, but in all of them and in everyone it is the same God at work.

> Now to each one the manifestation of the Spirit is given for the common good. To one there is given through the Spirit a message of wisdom, to another a message of knowledge by means of the same Spirit, to another faith by the same Spirit, to another gifts of healing by that one Spirit, to another miraculous powers, to another prophecy, to another

distinguishing between spirits, to another speaking in different kinds of tongues, and to still another the interpretation of tongues (1 Corinthians 12:7-10).

What is your spiritual gift? How are you using it? What are the spiritual gifts of your family members? How are you encouraging them to use their gifts?

Walking Our Dogs

I walked my dog the other day. It's something I do each day, sort of a ritual. It's almost an unspoken agreement we have with each another. It's important for both of us. It's our time of contact and connection. If I miss our time together, I feel I've let Shadow down and feel a bit guilty. Isn't that strange? Perhaps it's because I know how much it means to him. Each day he waits at the appointed time. His mouth and body quivers when he sees me coming. He shakes. He whines. He talks. It seems like the high point of his day—and perhaps it is. I even have to be careful with the word "walk." I've learned to spell it instead of saying it or he thinks we're going out immediately. Just recently, though, it appears he's learned to spell!

When it's time for a walk, Shadow lets me know. Once I let him out of his yard, he runs around in circles, a big, wild grin on his face. I say "leash," and he runs over and grabs the leash and then brings it directly to me. Once I have it, putting it on can be difficult because he's so excited.

What's my excitement level? I used to think a walk was a walk. But our walks have changed me. I've learned when we walk to be alert. Why? Sometimes there's a cat lurking in the bushes near our house. One day I was daydreaming when Shadow saw the cat. Immediately 75 pounds of dog was off running. I was pulled off my feet and bumped along the ground behind him. The worst part? Two neighbors saw the whole thing and love to remind me of who was walking whom that day!

One of the benefits of our walks is exercise—staying in shape for both of us. Some days we do a fast walk—3 ½ miles per hour. After a block of that, I usually start getting some looks from Shadow meaning, "Slow it down. I want to sniff and smell and mark my territory." One thing I don't enjoy is carrying that little bag and picking up Shadow's droppings. Remember, the larger the dog, the larger the pile. It's a little embarrassing when I meet a neighbor and wave at him or her, forgetting what I'm holding in my hand. I solved that problem finally. I have Shadow do his business *before* we walk. He's trained to go on command. I say either "Number One" or signal with one finger or I say "Number Two" or hold up two fingers. (I trained both dogs by catching them in the act, announcing the correct "number," and holding up the right amount of fingers. It was pure association, and fairly easy to teach them the commands.)

Of course, I'm not the only one walking. Do you wonder what Shadow thinks about on our walks?

"Shadow, do you like our walks? What do you think about them?" I asked my pup. Here's his reply.

Walks—yeah—I love them. New scenery. It's a great break from my yard. Sometimes it's boring staying in that old yard. That's one of the reasons I often dig or chew. I need variety too, you know. I need a break. Oh! What is that smell. Wow! Another dog walked by this morning! Oh, sorry. I got distracted. That's one of the reasons I like to walk *ssslllooooow-www*. Sometimes my guy goes too fast. I want and need to explore my neighborhood. I want to smell new smells and see new sights. Oh, somebody dropped a pizza slice! Boy, pepperoni and mushrooms! Great! Now, where was I?

I get a lot of attention when we walk, especially if we go down a new street or to the mall. Oh, look at those doves! I'm going to catch them! Darn, they got away. Why did Norm jerk on my chain? Now, where was I again?

Oh yes. Hey, these walks don't just benefit me. They've done wonders for my servant. Yeah, Norm thinks he owns and trains me, but it's the other way around. Let me tell you how it's done. The first thing I did was teach him to stay at heel when we walk. I had him hook one end of my leash to my collar and then loop the other end around his hand so he can't get away from me. Then I started walking down the street slowly, stopping at every tree, pole, or fire hydrant until he realized he's under control by me.

Oh sure, he tugged and yanked the leash at first, but I discouraged that by skipping between his legs and wrapping the leash around his ankles. Then I pulled hard. He hated that. When he tried to run ahead, I braced all four feet and came to an abrupt halt. Boy, did that work! He landed flat on his back. A few times of that and now he follows my lead.

And that myth of him teaching me to go potty on command? Ha! Don't believe it. I taught him to say those words and give those ridiculous signals so he'd have something to talk about with his friends while I run around.

Anyway, walking has been good for my guy. Now he takes the time to notice his surroundings—animals, birds, cats, flowers, the changing color of tree leaves. That last one is kind of weird, but what can I say. He's my guy. He talks to me about them all the time.

One of the big benefits for him is all the people he's met that he never knew. Yes, I'm a people magnet. Sometimes it takes three times as long to walk because of Norm stopping to talk to people. That's OK because I usually get a big hug or a vigorous rub. I love that.

Hey, do you walk your dog? Maybe we'll meet someday so we can play together!

Walking has many purposes. Some walking in life is random, and some is purposeful. The word "walk" is used many times in Scripture.

Have you ever looked in a concordance at all the verses with "walk" in them? It's an amazing study that will bless and encourage you. Here are a few.

> Those who hope in the LORD will renew their strength. They will soar on wings like eagles; they will run and not grow weary, they will walk and not be faint (Isaiah 40:31).

> If we live by the [Holy] Spirit, let us also walk by the Spirit. [If by the Holy Spirit we have our life in God, let us go forward walking in line, our conduct controlled by the Spirit] (Galatians 5:25 AMP, brackets in original).

> Walk in the way of love, just as Christ loved us and gave himself up for us as a fragrant offering and sacrifice to God (Ephesians 5:2).

> Look carefully then how you walk! Live purposefully and worthily and accurately, not as the unwise and witless, but as wise (sensible, intelligent people) (5:15 AMP, parentheses in original).

> Walk (live and conduct yourselves) in a manner worthy of the Lord, fully pleasing to Him and desiring to please Him in all things, bearing fruit in every good work and steadily growing and increasing in and by the knowledge of God [with fuller, deeper, and clearer insight, acquaintance, and recognition] (Colossians 1:10 AMP, brackets in original).

> We beg and admonish you in [virtue of our union with] the Lord Jesus, that [you follow the instructions which] you learned from us about how you ought to walk so as to please and gratify God, as indeed you are doing, [and] that you do so even more and more abundantly [attaining yet greater perfection in living this life] (1 Thessalonians 4:1 AMP, brackets in original).

In those few verses we have the promise of not becoming weary.

We are told to walk by faith, walk by the Holy Spirit, walk in love, be careful about our walk, walk in a way that reflects Jesus in our lives, and to please God in the way we walk. The Christian life is indeed a walk, a process, and there are guidelines found in the Bible for this journey. The way we walk reflects our relationship with God as well as a way to draw others to Him.

How is your walk? Are you walking through life alone or with God? Jesus knew about walking. He walked with His friends, with the hurting, with the hopeless, and with the outcasts. And one day He walked, in the midst of crowds and soldiers and religious officials. He walked as He carried a cross. He stumbled on His walk, but He kept moving until He could barely move. Even when the guards ordered someone else to carry the cross for Him, Jesus walked beside him. He wouldn't quit. He had a destination—Golgotha. And He wasn't just walking for Himself. He was walking to the cross for you and me and everyone. His was a walk of redemption. A purposeful walk. A walk that was a gift for the entire world.

Hallelujah! Thank You, Lord Jesus!

Going Fishing

I went shore fishing the other day and took a friend with me. In fact, I went more for him than for me. He hadn't been fishing in a while. You see, he's getting old. He's finding it harder to get around, and his hearing is going. He was quite excited when I told him we were going to the lake. I knew the shore would be easier for him than sitting in my old junker boat I keep at the reservoir.

When we arrived, we walked on an old, weed-filled road and headed toward the dam because bass had been schooling there recently. I was bent on getting out there to fish, but my companion seemed to want to take his time. He stopped and noticed the foliage and paid close attention to the wildlife around us. I took a cue from him and slowed down to see what I'd been missing.

When we finally got to the dam, we sat down, and I began casting out over the sloping bank. I alternated between a purple worm and a great fleck Yamamoto spider jig. My friend just sat on a towel, content as he watched me catch and release a dozen bass and rattle on about nothing significant. I probably repeated stories he'd heard before, but it didn't bother him like it does some people. Now and then he'd get up and come over to take a closer look at a bass I'd caught. He's seen many fish in his time. In fact, he's even had some slap him in the head as I lifted them into the boat. He took it all in stride.

As we walked the half mile back to the car, I noticed how much his pace had slowed. He seemed weary, and it was more of an effort to get into the van. I told him to just rest while we drove back to my house. We didn't need to talk. I wondered how many more times he'd be able to go fishing with me. I guess I'd taken it for granted that we'd always be able to go fishing together. Have you ever wondered about that? Most people assume nothing will change. I know that one day my friend won't be able to go. I don't look forward to that day at all.

My friend is an excellent sight fisherman. He can spot a bass near the shoreline or next to a rock that I've missed. And he'll stay focused on that fish until it's caught. What's great about him is that he usually gives me the first opportunity to catch it. Once in a while he gets a bit impatient and goes for it himself. He's also got an uncanny ability to spot crawdads and other critters under the water.

I've learned a lot from him these last few years, and I've still got more to learn. My fishing buddy has touched my life in other ways as well. He came into my life about eight months after my son, Matthew, died. For my wife and me, this new friend was a source of comfort during our journey through grief. But we aren't the only ones he helped. A few years later when my mom was spending her last two months in a convalescent home, I'd visit each day and take my friend with me. He connected so well with Mom and the other residents that some of them would sit in the lobby for hours waiting to see him. And when they did, their faces, which most of the time had very little expression, would brighten and rare smiles would emerge. Several would congregate around him. His gentle touch and quiet presence brought delight, comfort, and a bright spot into their days of drab routine. He'd smile at each one and either put his head or a paw in their laps.

Sometimes I'd share stories with them about how my friend would stalk turtles or crawdads in my small backyard pond. One day he was putting his head under the water up to his ears, so I put a snorkel on him and took a series of pictures. They all laughed at the thought of a 75-pound golden retriever wearing a snorkel.

A dog for a friend? Oh, yes! Sheffield was more faithful, loyal, patient, and fun-loving than a lot of people I know. And he never tired of going fishing with me. My loving companion got cancer, but he seemed to rally after treatment. Then Christmas came, and after the holiday each day became more difficult for him.

His last day started out as any other day. Sheffield raised his head to look around, but then he slowly lowered it back to the ground. He thumped his tail a couple of times in greeting, but even that seemed to be a huge effort. When he did finally get up, he just stood there as though in a daze. Later that morning, I called him to the front door to see if he wanted to go out and get the paper, his usual routine. He took a few faltering steps, and then he hesitated, as if he didn't know which direction to go. Slowly he moved to the paper, lowered his head, and picked it up. He barely made it to the door before he stopped. He seemed totally exhausted. Finally, he gave his tail a wag and dropped the paper.

Sheffield had retrieved the paper thousands of times through the years, and he always brought it in to me with a visible sense of pride. Sometimes when he approached the paper, he would stop and look up and down the street just to see who was watching. The only day of the week that he grumped a bit about the task was on Sundays. On that day, the *Los Angeles Times* usually weighed more than seven pounds! But he always came through, just like he did today. Sadly, we both knew it would be the last time.

That evening I sent him out to the yard to relieve himself. When he got outside, he just lay down and rested his head on his paws. He seemed immobile. I walked out and helped him back toward the house. He flopped down on the deck, his breathing ragged and short. My wife and I thought he might die right there. But he rallied and eventually walked to the room where he usually slept.

The next morning his breathing was worse, and he could only walk a few feet. For as long as I can remember, Sheffield always came into my study in the morning to be with me while I had my devotions. This morning I reversed the procedure. I brought my Bible and devotional books into his room, sat on the floor next to him, placed one hand on his back, and then read and prayed. It was a difficult time because I knew what was coming, but it was also a special time.

My wife and I knew we needed to take him to the vet. We placed Sheffield on a towel and lifted him into the van. When we arrived, two of the vet's assistants brought out a gurney, placed him on it, and took him in. We waited in one of the rooms, and almost immediately the vet came in to tell us Sheffield was just about gone. The vet said he could prolong my friend's life for a brief time, if we wanted. We said, "No, we know it's time to let go."

Sheffield and I had been saying goodbye for several days, but I went in for a final farewell. I'm not sure if he was conscious or not. There was a tube down his throat, and it was apparent he would be gone within a few minutes. I gently rubbed his back and head and said goodbye.

December 31 that year was one of the longest days of my life. Just as the memories of a significant person who is gone elicit tears, so do pictures and memories of Sheffield.

In Loving Memory
River Pines Flame of Sheffield
September 3, 1990–December 31, 2002

I was blessed with so many understanding friends during that time. The flowers and cards I received validated my feelings that Sheffield had touched the lives of more people than I knew. He taught me about friendship, faithfulness, loyalty, patience, and love.

I thank God for Sheffield being a member of my family. I still miss him greatly.

Dream On

Your dog is stretched out on the floor, not a care, and dead to the world. You wonder how he does it—turning off everything and being so peaceful. And then it begins. At first he quivers in his hind legs and then the front. Now they're twitching almost rhythmically. You hear a growl, and it even sounds a bit painful. Now he snaps his jaws, and you figure he's chasing some sleep-created beast or rabbit. What's going on? It's doggy dreams. Yes, dogs dream. I've always wanted some type of machine that would project my dog's dreams onto a screen. During sleep, a dog's brain-wave patterns follow much the same time course as people's. They go through the same sleep stages we do.

Some researchers say there is evidence that not only do dogs dream, but they dream about common dog activities. The studies showed that dogs started to move only when their brains entered the stage of sleep associated with dreaming. The author of *How Dogs Think* wrote:

> During the course of a dream episode these dogs actually began to execute the actions that they were performing in their dreams. Thus researchers found that a dreaming pointer may immediately start searching for game and even go on point, a sleeping Springer spaniel may flush an imaginary bird in his dreams, while a dreaming Doberman pinscher may pick a fight with a dream burglar.

It is really quite easy to determine when your dog is dreaming. All that you have to do is watch him from the time he starts to doze off. As the dog's sleep becomes deeper, his breathing will become more regular. After a period of about twenty minutes for an average-sized dog, his first dream should start. You can recognize the change because his breathing will become shallow and irregular. There may be odd muscle twitches, and you may even see the dog's eyes moving behind its closed lids if you look closely enough. The eyes are moving because the dog is actually looking at the dream images as if they were real images of the world. The eye movements are the most obvious characteristics of dreaming sleep. When human beings are awakened during this rapid eye movement, or REM, sleep, they virtually always report that they were dreaming.[1]

Do all dogs dream the same? No. Different types of dogs have different patterns of dreaming. Who dreams more frequently— large dogs or small dogs? What do you think? Do certain breeds dream more because they are highly active and are used to doing more than some dogs who tend to sit or lie around all day? I didn't find any research on breeds and dreams, but I did find some on size. Small dogs dream more frequently than large dogs. A toy poodle, for instance, may dream once every 10 minutes while a large dog, such as a Great Dane or Irish wolfhound, may go an hour or two between dreams.

Sometimes I just sit and watch my golden retrievers lie there and dream. When one of them twitches and then moans and groans like something intense or terrible is going on, I wonder whether I should do something. Do I wake him or not? Do I let him dream on? Usually I figure dreaming doesn't hurt anything, so I let him dream on. One time when Aspen was dreaming, I said his name. "Aspen." No response. "Aspen," I said a bit louder. Still no response. Finally in a loud voice I said, "Aspen!"

Aspen's body jerked. He opened his eyes and looked around as if saying, "Hey! What's happenin'? What's going on? Huh?"

I think he looked embarrassed, although I'm not sure dogs get embarrassed. Then Aspen looked at me, sighed, rolled over, and went back to sleep.

Do the dreams of dogs follow the pattern of people in other ways? Yes, they do. Just as we do, the amount of time dogs spend dreaming depends on their age. Younger dogs spend much more time dreaming than older dogs.[2]

We all dream. Sometimes we remember them and sometimes we don't. Some dreams are pleasant, and some aren't. Some bring peace, while others bring fear. Sometimes we wish we'd dream about a loved one who has died, and on other occasions we'd prefer not to.

We also all daydream. What do you dream about consciously for your life? Have you asked God to give you a dream that would fulfill you and glorify Him? It's worth doing.

Sometimes God speaks to us through dreams. We've seen this in Scripture, especially in the lives of two Josephs—one mentioned in the Old Testament and one mentioned in the New Testament (for instance, see Genesis 37 and Matthew 1).

Sometimes our sleep is troubled and disrupted because of our dreams. If you experience that, I have a suggestion. Just before you turn out the light, commit your time of sleep to the Lord through prayer. Ask Him to speak to you, to give you rest, to give you freedom from conflicted dreams, and to help you feel refreshed. Pray something similar to this:

Dear God,

We give thanks for the darkness of the night where lies the world of dreams. Guide us closer to our dreams so that we may be nourished by them. Give us good dreams and memory of them so that we may carry their poetry and mystery into our daily lives.

Grant us deep and restful sleep that we may wake refreshed with strength enough to renew a world grown tired.

We give thanks for the inspiration of stars, the dignity of the moon and the lullabies of crickets and frogs.

Let us restore the night and reclaim it as a sanctuary of peace, where silence shall be music to our hearts and darkness shall throw light upon our souls. Good night. Sweet dreams. Amen.[3]

Now, finish by reading these Scriptures out loud. You may be surprised at the difference this can make.

When you lie down, you shall not be afraid; yes, you shall lie down, and your sleep shall be sweet. Be not afraid of sudden terror and panic, nor of the stormy blast or the storm and ruin of the wicked when it comes [for you will be guiltless], for the Lord shall be your confidence, firm and strong, and shall keep your foot from being caught [in a trap or hidden danger] (Proverbs 3:24-26 AMP, brackets in original).

I lay down and slept in peace and woke up safely, for the Lord was watching over me (Psalm 3:5 TLB).

If I'm sleepless at midnight, I spend the hours in grateful reflection (63:6 MSG).

When my anxious thoughts multiply within me, Your consolations delight my soul (94:19 NASB).

In peace I will lie down and sleep, for you alone, LORD, make me dwell in safety (4:8).

In a dream, a vision of the night, when sound sleep falls on men, while they slumber in their beds, then [God] opens the ears of men, and seals their instruction (Job 33:15-16 NASB).

George the Pest

A pest. There is no better word to describe George. Who names a dog "George" anyway? He really was something. When he liked someone, he really liked him or her. And he was likable too, all right. It's just that when he liked you, he became intrusive and a bit obnoxious. He was harmless, but he sometimes lacked social skills, good sense, or an understanding of boundaries. He was an irritation—or at least what he did was irritating. But a person couldn't help but like him. He was the kind of dog people tried to avoid at times. If he was sleeping, we'd try to walk quietly or tiptoe around him so he wouldn't wake up and greet us with unleashed enthusiasm.

I remember my first experience with George. It was at a rural retreat center near Fallbrook, California. I'd met him the night before and played with him. That's another thing about George. It was hard to wear him out, but that's pretty common with dogs who are addicted to tennis balls. The next day was a beautiful morning, and I was enjoying myself during a walk in the woods. I noticed a small opening in the forest. I also noticed a smell that wasn't just not pleasant, it stunk to the high heavens. Coming closer, I saw a soggy pile of something on the ground—and George was rolling around in it. At least I thought it was him. The night before he was a beautiful Weimaraner with a rich, gray coat. The dog in front of me had some gray, but there were more hunks of black sticky stuff than gray. And the dog reeked.

Then it happened. George must have heard me, so he stopped, looked around, got to his feet, and stared at me. I froze. I knew what he was about to do. His short tail wagged, his body shook, and he began to whimper with excitement. I knew what he was thinking, and I wanted nothing to do with stinky George.

I turned and ran.

So did George.

I ran faster.

So did he.

I'm sure he thought it was a great game. Fortunately, I got to the old barn first. I ran in one door with George close behind me. Then I ran out another door, shutting it quickly, and ran around and closed the first door. I could still smell him, but now he couldn't reach me. I know he liked me, but I sure didn't want to smell like him right then!

I found out George also had a great memory. I was at the same retreat center a few months later and asked (with mixed emotions), "Is George still here?" "Oh, yes," was the reply. "In fact, I think he missed you. He'll be glad to see you." I said, "Oh great!" meaning, "I hope he's cleaned up!"

One of the unique features at this retreat center was a cable bridge. It was probably 200 feet long and stretched across a small ravine so it was close to 85 feet above the ground. It swayed and bumped when someone walked slowly across, but it was actually quite safe. When more than one person walked across at the same time, it was important to walk in sync, putting the same feet down at the same time to lessen the side-to-side and up-and-down swaying. The more out of sync you were, the worse the sway, which made walking quite difficult.

On this day, the usually safe walk across became a risky adventure. I was walking across, and looked up at the other side. My heart sank. It was my friend George. And he looked happy—tail wagging, mouth open, body wiggling. I was sure he didn't understand cable bridges. He saw me and wanted to greet me—that's all that mattered to him. He took a step onto the bridge and then tried to lope toward me. Loping isn't a good idea on a cable bridge!

The direction I was walking was on an incline. George loped faster. I tried to turn around and go back, but the bridge had other plans. By now it was swaying, gyrating, and bouncing. It moved side to side and up and down. I couldn't stand up anymore. It was like an earthquake and tornado mixed together. I fell. Fortunately, so did George. He was about 10 feet away, and he actually looked panicked. His legs went every which way. He tried to stand, and with the bridge swaying and bouncing it didn't work. Naturally, by now we'd drawn a crowd—a laughing crowd. To save myself from George's friendly onslaught, I did the best thing I could do. I crawled off the bridge and went into the house. The last I saw of George he was still trying to get his footing.

That night George entered my life again. The men slept in an old-style bunkhouse on bunk beds. George had been following me all day, wanting attention. During meetings he lay down on my feet and slept. He drooled on my shoe when I ate lunch. He sometimes tripped me when I went on a walk. But now it was nighttime, and I felt safe in my upper bunk as I settled in to get a good night's sleep. It didn't happen that way.

It was a cold night—quite cold—but it was toasty and comfortable in my sleeping bag. For me, that is. George was outside. He didn't like being outside, and he didn't like the cold. About every 45 seconds he'd yip and moan. Then there'd be silence. Then he'd yip and moan again. This happened over and over until some "wise" individual let him in the bunkhouse.

Of course he sought me out. He climbed onto the lower bunk right under me, which happened to be empty. And then he was quiet. But he was still cold. How do I know that? Because as I lay there trying my best to go to sleep, I couldn't. Why? George. Every 30 seconds or so he shivered. And not just a small shiver—a big one. The entire bunk-bed structure shook. Yes, I know he was cold, but...After a half an hour of this and hoping he'd get warm, I got up and took him to the house. I opened the door and let him inside where it was nice and warm. I'd had my fill of George for one day.

Can you relate? Do you know people like George? Sometimes we get our fill of certain people. They're intrusive, fail to respect boundaries, and don't enhance our lives. They interfere and disrupt. They're irritating. This reminds me of some people descriptions in the book of Proverbs:

> Like one who takes away a garment on a cold day, or like vinegar poured on a wound, is one who sings songs to a heavy heart (25:20).

> Do you see a person wise in their own eyes? There is more hope for a fool than for them (26:12).

> Like a maniac shooting flaming arrows of death is one who deceives their neighbor and says, "I was only joking!" (26:18-19).

> If you shout a pleasant greeting to a friend too early in the morning, he will count it as a curse (27:14 TLB).

Sometimes we look at passages like these, smile, and say, "Oh, yeah. I've run into people like that." I personally think they're like human versions of George. Perhaps our next thought should be, "I hope I'm not like those people or George! I hope I'm not irritating to others." And then we should make sure we're not.

Hidden or Found?

Remember the games you played as a child? I'm sure you played Hide-and-Seek. It's an interesting game since you're hiding to be found. Some kids get very creative in where they hide. We adults sometimes do the same in various ways. Sometimes when we're found, it's a bit disastrous. A number of us were counselors at a high school camp, and the campers wanted to play "Counselor Hunt." We had five minutes to hide somewhere on the grounds, and then 200 kids started searching. I was determined not to be found so I'd win. I went behind the cafeteria where they had huge garbage cans. I found one that was both empty and clean. I quickly gathered a number of newspapers, jumped in, and spread the papers over me so if anyone looked in the can, it would appear as if there was just trash inside. Time went by, and I heard kids run by. One opened the lid but all he saw was "trash," so he moved on. More time went by, and I was just about ready to get out and sneak up to the winner's stand when I heard a door close and footsteps approach. The lid came off, and someone (probably the cook) dropped a large glob of lunch remains into the garbage can. I remained quiet as the garbage seeped through the paper and covered me from head to toe. At that point I wished I'd been found already! I looked like garbage. I smelled like garbage. I think I became garbage.

After I got out and cleaned up, I noticed that several other counselors who were very creative and usually weren't found had already been apprehended. I wondered how this happened until I noticed a kid sitting nearby with his arms wrapped around a hound dog. Both he and the dog were grinning, and I knew with that dog around no one could safely hide for long.

Recently I found the delightful book *What My Dog Has Taught Me About Life—Meditations for Dog Lovers.* One of the dogs the author talked about was a Lab by the name of Griffin. The author spent 18 months raising Griffin as a future guide dog and then went through the agony of letting the pup go back to the Guide Dog Organization. But then he received a call that Griffin didn't qualify as a guide dog because of potential hip dysplasia. They said that when it got bad, Griffin might have to be put down. When the author brought him home, the dog's bones must have calcified because he remained pain free and lived another 10 years! Here's another one of the stories from that book for you to enjoy.

Little kids love to hide in order to be found. Not so with dogs. Dogs hide *not* to be found. Run some water in the bathtub, and bring in a few extra towels, and some dog shampoo. ZOOM! Griff goes into hiding every time. How does he know?

Call. Cajole. Command. It's pretty much a waste of time. He won't come. You have to go and find him. Usually, he's hiding under the dining-room table, in the far corner of the living room, or behind Luci.

Reluctant to the bone, Griff delays, retreats, rolls on his back with paws tight to his chest. He's a blob of defeat, seeking mercy from a prone, penitent position. Poor, pathetic thing!

"What's the big deal? It's only a bath! And you really need one."

The thing is, when it's all over, Griffin is in his most celebratory mood. Toweled down, shaken off, free to roam, he runs through the house. And from somewhere deep inside, he resonates the most contented sound known in dogdom, "GGRRAAAUGHH!"

Griffin isn't the only one who hides so he won't be found. I'm prone to do some hiding of my own come bath time. When life gets messy and I'm losing control, it's hard not to hide.

We both like life to run in comfortable and predictable patterns. We both tolerate a considerable amount of personal messiness without feeling the need to be clean. We both like to sort things out on our own with little outside interference. Griffin has little talent for hiding. I wish I could say the same for me.

I have many layers I can hide behind—masks of my own making. Just ask Luci. She'll tell you that masquerades often aren't the "ball" they're touted to be. She hates masks—mine and hers.

Somehow I get the notion that the real me isn't good enough. It isn't safe to come out of hiding. I doubt the motives of anyone who comes looking for me with anything looking like a washrag.

It has been that way from the very beginning. The first questions asked of the first man was, "Where are you?" Adam, hiding not to be found, was found out. The best thing that could have happened to him after his forbidden snack was for God to say, "Bath time, Adam! You really need one. Stop slinking around. Once you're clean you'll feel like dancing."

In the notable poem by Francis Thompson, "The Hound of Heaven" chases us down the corridors of time, sniffs us out, dogs our days, and we flee from God in terror. We hide in darkness. Then one day, with nowhere to turn, no mask within reach, we face our lifelong hunter. The Hound of Heaven approaches, and not to devour our souls, but to wash our feet and make us clean.[1]

What If Your Dog Could Pray?

Have you ever wondered what your dog would pray about? Most of us probably haven't. We have better things to do with our time and thoughts. I found a unique book titled *Dog Psalms: Prayers My Dog Has Taught Me* by Herbert Brokering. These unique prayers reflect some of the attributes of dogs. Some of the topics are:

• I wiggle	• I hope	• I growl	• I snuggle
• I guard	• I hunt	• I work	• I bluff
• I watch	• I chase	• I forgive	• I nudge
• I wait	• I dig	• I stray	• I heal

In each of these writings, a dog tells about himself in terms of what he will do, which sounds a bit like a psalm. And then he prays, which again sounds like a psalm. What does this dog psalm titled "I wiggle" say to you?

I am a dog. I love you. My whole being shows you my affection. With eyes and lips and paws and tongue, I love you. I assume with my whole self that you love me too. I wiggle and wag and jump and climb and pant for you to love me. I am dog. I feel innocent even after proven guilty. I love you unconditionally, believing you love me the same. I am dog. The tides of the oceans are in me. I wiggle as I ride waves, hear love calls of ancient forests, feel the kiss of a wisp of wind. I have a spirit that runs through all times.

God,

My spirit wiggles in me. I dance in my heart when I feel your closeness. I cannot hold my feelings still. Your spirit runs through me like a living stream, a slow rhythm, and with you I am young. You keep me alive with goodness from the earth and the heavens. You find the good in me. You move me with your joy.[1]

Isn't that an amazing psalm? Yes, our dogs love us. But that's nothing compared to the love God has for us and has given to us through His Son, Jesus Christ. Have you ever wiggled in anticipation of spending time with God? Have you ever felt the sentiment behind the line, "I wiggle and wag and jump and climb and pant for you to love me"? Why not let the elation and delight of this dog challenge you to consider how fresh and vibrant your relationship is with the Lord?

Waiting is another attribute highlighted in *Dog Psalms*. Have you thought about how much of his lifetime a dog spends waiting? Think about it. Waiting to be fed, waiting to go on a walk, waiting to play ball. Listen to this dog.

I am dog. I am patient. I can be taught to wait. I do not prefer to wait in a long line. I want to be the only dog waiting. If you are coming, I will wait, breathing deeply, half dreaming, wholly wishing. When I know you love me I live for you with every breath. I bury my yearning deep inside and hide it in my sleeplessness. I toss and turn and wait until you are here. I wait for you sometimes while singing, sometimes while whimpering, howling, wanting with all my heart. I can wait loud or soft. I can wait through long night watches. I will wait without end, knowing I am wanted. I am dog, willing, patient. Waiting prepares me for your presence.

God,

You have given me the gift of waiting. Like a child, I wait with my whole body, mind and soul. I wait for seasons, they go; I wait for another, it comes. I wait for days to dawn, nights to darken, seeds to break open, fruit to fall. As I wait I learn the gift of patience and the joy of surprise. While I wait I find myself in your presence. I wait for you, and in waiting I see you are here, waiting.[2]

How do you do with waiting? Much of our lives are spent doing just that—waiting. For many of us we consider it an irritant, a pain, a waste of time. The ability to wait is developed through the character qualities or fruit of the Holy Spirit: "The fruit of the Spirit is love, joy, peace, *patience*, kindness, goodness, faithfulness, gentleness, self-control" (Galatians 5:22-23 NASB). Many of us pray for patience this way: "Lord, give me patience *right* now." We don't even have the patience to pray and wait for patience! Sometimes we tell our dogs to wait, and we can tell they don't want to. I'll put food in Shadow's bowl and say, "Wait." He waits, but every muscle is tense and he's quivering and drooling. Is that real waiting? No. Waiting is relaxing and resting and enjoying the moment until fruition comes, especially when waiting involves God. The psalmist knew this. He calls us to wait on the Lord:

Guide me in Your truth and faithfulness and teach me, for You are the God of my salvation; for You [You only and altogether] do I wait [expectantly] all the day long (Psalm 25:5 AMP, brackets in original).

Wait for the LORD; be strong and take heart and wait for the LORD (27:14).

Be still before the LORD and wait patiently for him; do not fret when people succeed in their ways, when they carry out their wicked schemes (37:7).

Wait for and expect the Lord and keep and heed His way, and He will exalt you to inherit the land; [in the end] when the wicked are cut off, you shall see it (37:34 AMP, brackets in original).

When they see me waiting, expecting your Word, those who fear you will take heart and be glad (119:74 MSG).

You're my place of quiet retreat; I wait for your Word to renew me (119:114 MSG).

Do you wait like the psalm-writing dog does? Read the second psalm again. He anticipates and eagerly looks forward to his encounter. Can you say to God like he does, "I am your child, willing, patient"? Can you say, "Waiting prepares me for your presence"? Take a few minutes and sit in a quiet place. Every several seconds say out loud, "Lord, waiting prepares me for Your presence. Speak to me. Be close to me." You may be surprised at the outcome. God may speak to you through your mind or His Word. Just wait.

By the way, if I asked your dog how to pray for you, what would he say? It's kind of a strange idea, I know, but think about it for a minute. What do you need to be prayed for at this time in your life?

Sometimes I've heard people share more openly and honestly with their dog than they do with other people. They feel more secure and safe. They don't feel they have to put on a pretense or deal with someone giving a lot of advice, not listening, or being critical in response. Let's face it: Dogs are great listeners. You can say the same thing over and over again, and it doesn't bother your dog. He just listens and accepts you. He's happy that you're taking the time to share with him.

And isn't that sort of like how God responds to you when you're talking? Have you experienced this? He's here waiting for you, wanting to hear from you, yearning for you to invite Him in for a chat.

Good Intentions

I remember the day well. I was on a field trip in college. We were going to visit a hospital, and I was wearing a pair of white pants known at the time as "duck" pants. My car was loaded with other students, and we stopped to get some Cokes. Since I was driving, I couldn't hold the drink so I gripped it between my teeth. When I wanted some, I simply tilted my head back and let the liquid trickle down my throat. Everything went well until the girl next to me put her hand over, as if she were going to tap the cup that was in my mouth, threatening to make me spill it. I responded by opening my mouth to say, "Don't you dare do that!" You can imagine what happened! When I opened my mouth, the cup fell out and the contents, including the ice, splashed out and ran all over my white ducks. I was soaked and uncomfortable, but everyone else in the car loved my dilemma and laughed. (Way too much, in my opinion.)

The first thing I did when I arrived back at the dorm was change out of the still-damp white ducks and put on another pair of identical trousers. (Yes, I must have really liked this color and style.) I did some errands around the campus, and then I went back to my room.

I decided to clean up the college-life debris scattered all over. When I squatted down to lift a large box of papers, I felt something give and heard a tearing sound. Yep, I'd ripped my pants. And it wasn't just a slight rip—it was massive. I could already feel the draft hitting my skin. I couldn't repair this damage, so once again I had to change my pants. Yep, I put on my remaining pair of white ducks. I thought, "Two out of three ruined. Surely that's enough for one day." These pants were clean and larger, so I didn't have to worry about them ripping.

Enter Beowulf. He was a large, white dog. Did I say large? He was massive! And he was overly friendly. No one knew where he came from or who might own him. He was just around. He always seemed to be nearby. Sometimes invited; sometimes not invited. He had a pretty good life since he was a gregarious, happy, friendly, extroverted dog. When the weather was warm and a class met outside on the lawn, he invited himself to sit in and listen, becoming one of the students. He usually ended up getting numerous snacks and plenty of attention, plus he didn't have to take any exams. When he was really hungry, he had a great routine. He would sit outside the dining hall and whimper (who could refuse that?) or he would go to the garbage cans and wait for someone to bring out a container of leftovers. He was certainly well fed!

He liked me. I'm sure of it. When he saw me, he'd break away from others and run to greet me. That was usually fine—but not on this day. When I walked out of the dorm room and saw him, he also saw me. He'd been in the dirt. He'd been in the mud. I could see mud stains going six inches up each leg. Two hundred feet separated us, and he immediately ran toward me. I could see mud and saliva flying through the air. Beowulf's tail was wagging. He was delighted to see me and wanted to shower his love and affection on me.

Any day, but today! I thought. I tried to backtrack and get away, but I wasn't fast enough. He rushed up to me, jumped up, and his dirty front paws pressed against my chest. As I backed away, his paws slid down onto my pant legs. Now I had two-inch-wide black streaks down each pant leg. Yep, my ducks were now black and white.

I looked at the enormous dog and said, "How could you?"

He looked at me as if saying, "It was easy. I love you and wanted to greet you!"

Yes, he had good intentions but the results were disastrous for me.

He walked away happy and oblivious to his negative impact. My friends and fellow students were enjoying this episode and actually applauding the four-legged beast.

Beowulf's response reminds me how many of us have good intentions but end up with wrong results. Sometimes what we say to be helpful has the opposite effect. I try to take this proverb to heart. Can you relate? "Don't talk so much. You keep putting your foot in your mouth. Be sensible and turn off the flow!" (Proverbs 10:19 TLB). Sometimes we think our detailed advice is what a family member or friend needs, but perhaps it's not. Fewer words are often better than going on and on. It also gives us more opportunities to think about what we're going to say instead of just blurting out something. Here is more wisdom from the book of Proverbs, Amplified version:

> The tongue of the wise utters knowledge rightly, but the mouth of the [self-confident] fool pours out folly (15:2).

> A man has joy in making an apt answer, and a word spoken at the right moment—how good it is! (15:23).

> He who has knowledge spares his words, and a man of understanding has a cool spirit. Even a fool when he holds his peace is considered wise; when he closes his lips he is esteemed a man of understanding (17:27-28).

Most of us try to be helpful in what we do or what we say. We tend to think we know what is best for someone else. But do we really? It may be better and safer to let the other person know we're available and would like to help if he or she would like some. Another good question is to ask what they'd like us to say or do for them.

I'm a grief and trauma therapist. I sit with those grieving, usually at some of the most painful times of their lives. Many people have shared with me not only the pain of their loss but also the pain of what they've heard from others who attempted to offer comfort or tried to fix a situation. When a person is grieving, he or she doesn't need or want to be fixed. The person needs comfort. He or she needs the presence of people who will patiently come alongside and sit in silence or ask how they can help in even a simple or small way. Hurting people don't necessarily need us to fill the air with words. They need us to be present. To be with them. So before we act on our good intentions, let's pray for God's wisdom and guidance. And then we can move forward, asking the grieving person, "What would be the most helpful for you right now?" The answer may be just our loving presence.

The next time your good intentions are about to kick in, remember Beowulf and my white duck pants.

Dog Truths or Myths?

There are many beliefs about dogs. Some are true, some are possible, some are myths. The latter category abounds with information, and many dog owners believe them. What about you? Let's consider some common statements and test your knowledge.

Dogs respect those who feed them the most. True, possible, or false? It's false. Leadership is much more the basis of your relationship with your dog than food. It's the emotional alliance you make with your dog that makes the difference. This means the person who is most involved with training your dog creates the bond. So the best method is to have each family member involved in the training for the bonds to occur.

Dogs have no feelings. Did you name your dog "Mr. Spock"? Is your dog a robot? Your dog is put together like you are. Dogs have emotions and feelings. They experience love, anger, frustration, despair, depression, and hope, just to list a few emotions. I've met some dogs who are more in tune with their emotions than some people.

Dogs are animals so they belong outside. First of all, a dog is a pack animal, so he needs strong social bonds. They like being in families, not solitary confinement. Your dog needs time with you and your family, indoors and outdoors. Dogs who do without can become insecure as well as aggressive.

Dogs need lots of room, and large dogs need more space than others. Not true. Some small dogs need more exercise than large ones. You may have more preferences for space and where you live than your dog does. Large dogs can live in small city apartments as long as they get exercise and have quality time with you. Tennis balls thrown 20 times for him is preferred by your dog than having a half acre of land to run around in by himself.

You can't teach a dog new tricks. Older dogs are like older people. It may take a bit longer to learn and flexibility in our bodies may be less, but older creatures do focus better on learning and can draw on past knowledge to help. An older dog may not learn as fast as a puppy, but he can learn or unlearn practically anything.

Dogs who learn quickly are smarter than those who learn slowly. It's true! Speed of learning can indicate intelligence, but that's only one indicator. Different breeds and different dogs assimilate information at different rates. Often a dog that learns quickly can also discard it quickly, and a slower dog might be better at retaining what he's learned.

If my dog loves me, he will do everything I ask. Even people don't respond this way. Obedience comes more from training than love. It's important to teach your dog the response you want instead of what you don't want. I've seen too many people teach their dogs to be disobedient. If your dog doesn't come when called, could it be he was taught not to? Why would anyone do that? Let's say you called your dog to come to you and he doesn't. You call again with a more intense and firm voice. He comes, but when he arrives you scold him for not coming the first time. Your dog is not going to connect the scolding with the initial refusal. So your dog goes off thinking, "Why should I come? I just got scolded."

Dogs will get into trouble when their masters are away. Yes and no. Most of us have heard stories about a dog that devoured the interior of a house or a car. The dog wasn't malicious, and he didn't have a "destroy gene." He was bored! If you leave your dog alone for a period of time with nothing to do...watch out! He will find something to do! Children often are the same way. Spending extra dollars for dog toys is far cheaper than buying a new couch or dining room table.

Another idea is to not give your dog free run of the house. Establish his territory for him. Turn on a radio in his area so he has familiar sounds when he's alone. Give him sturdy, flexible toys. Remember a barking, digging, or chewing dog is often a bored dog. It helps to have a second dog for companionship and exercise. If you do, get them from separate litters with a bit of an age difference. Puppies from the same litter bond together, and some owners have found this makes it more difficult for the dogs to bond to people. It also helps to train them separately and out of sight of one another.

Purebreds are not as smart as mutts. This is a generalization. It's true that some breeds have been inbred so much there are undesirable physical and mental characteristics. As one dog trainer stated, "Whenever a dog's master calls the animal stupid, he or she has almost certainly failed to make the right kind of emotional commitment to training the pet. Lack of intelligence in the dog isn't the issue, lack of good training by the human is."[1]

When it comes to myths, people aren't immune. Men believe myths about women. Women believe myths about men. We believe myths about entertainers and famous individuals. We believe myths about other religions. And we may even believe some myths about our own Christian faith. What is the true source of our beliefs? Is it what others have written, said, or preached? It very well could be. Fortunately, we have a source for what we believe that we can trust, that we can count on—the Bible, God's Word. And it is sufficient for each of us:

> Every Scripture is God-breathed (given by His inspiration) and profitable for instruction, for reproof and conviction of sin, for correction of error and discipline in obedience, [and] for training in righteousness (in holy living, in conformity to God's will in thought, purpose, and action), so that the man of God may be complete and proficient, well fitted

and thoroughly equipped for every good work (2 Timothy 3:16-17 AMP).

How can a young person stay on the path of purity? By living according to your word. I seek you with all my heart; do not let me stray from your commands. I have hidden your word in my heart that I might not sin against you. Praise be to you, LORD; teach me your decrees. With my lips I recount all the laws that come from your mouth. I rejoice in following your statutes as one rejoices in great riches. I meditate on your precepts and consider your ways. I delight in your decrees; I will not neglect your word (Psalm 119:9-16).

God's Word is here for a purpose. It provides *truth*, not myth. It provides answers, not questions. It provides the best way to live. When you follow what it says, you can be confident you're following truth. I suggest you read the two Scripture passages again. Why not read them aloud every day for a month? They'll be your assurance for a lifetime.

A Wounded Healer

This is the story of Bucky, a golden retriever who was a wounded healer. Before being traumatized, Bucky was training to become an assistance dog. His previous owner had struck and kicked him often, which caused Bucky to suffer severe anxiety attacks. He was found to be too nervous and frightened to be an assistance dog, so he was pulled from the program.

Hoping to help rehabilitate him, Salvation Army Escondido Corps Officer Major David Ebel adopted the shy puppy. Eventually when Major Ebel went to visit patients at the hospital, he took Bucky with him. Here's how the major described what happened.

We received Bucky at eight months old. When I finally got Bucky home from the trainer, I was very concerned that he was still having lots of overt responses to anything that might spook him. A leaf blowing by may cause him to back up, then turn around and try to run away from the tiny distraction.

When we decided to go out to dinner, we chose a place about a mile away that would be calm and relaxed. As we went to sit down at one of the wrought-iron tables, I decided to make it easy on everyone, so I suggested that we all sit down and my wife could sit with both dogs while I got the food. As I dropped the leash for Bucky on the arm of the heavy chair, I tried to communicate to my wife to sit in that chair so he would feel secure. Instead, she didn't understand what I was trying to say and sat in a different chair. Bucky saw me walking away and tried to follow me, causing the metal chair to scrape on the cement patio. It scared him so badly that he immediately became hysterical and began a full-blown panic attack. Dragging the chair back and forth, Bucky was feeling chased by the chair…which made it worse.

I ran to his aid, held him down, and calmed him. After a minute or so (it felt like weeks in slow motion), one of the patrons from the restaurant who had seen what happened came out and grabbed the chair and unhooked Bucky. In less than five minutes Bucky was again coming back to normal.

At that moment I knew he needed me as much as I needed him. A bond was made.

Upon our arrival back to the Salvation Army Escondido Corps parking lot, I led Bucky from the car, planning to go into the building. Instead, Bucky began to tug and pull me very hard toward the opposite end of the lot. No matter what I said or did, he kept being so insistent that I decided to find out what he was so focused on.

As we continued back to the opposite corner of the lot, I noticed there was an old, rusty pickup truck near the door to Family Services (social services). Bucky was unrelenting until we came around the passenger door of the truck and I noticed an older lady loading pantry groceries into the truck.

"Excuse me," I said. "Are you okay?"

"Do I look all right to you?" came the weeping reply.

"I am Major David, and my wife and I are pastors here at The Salvation Army, and it seemed to me that there might be a problem."

"Well, my husband of 38 years left this morning, and then he called me to tell me he is leaving me. He left me all right… with our 35-year-old, special-needs son and no money in the bank—he took it all. He took the good car and left me this old hunting truck that has leaky tires and is low on gas. And when I called the bank to see how much is in there, they shared that the house payment hadn't been paid for three months and wanted to know when they could expect the money.

"So then I called the utility companies and got the same story.

"I need a knee and two hip replacements, and I have no insurance. I haven't been able to work for over five years. Now what am I going to do?" She paused. "By the way, how did you know to come talk to me?" she asked.

"My dog brought me over here," I replied.

"Oh! Even the dogs know I'm abandoned!"

We did all we could to provide assistance for the woman, and I praised God that Bucky had dragged me on the scene. What a coincidence!

In the next two months, Bucky discerned that there was a problem two more times…and he dragged me to meet someone I had yet to notice who was in serious need. No coincidence after all. It was divine appointment!

I've been a disaster responder for many years. As a fire chaplain, a Critical Incident Stress Management (disaster response mental health triage) responder, and then an incident commander and trainer, I was very concerned that if Bucky was to be with me constantly (as service dogs are trained to do), I needed him to be able to be compassionate and comforting with those who are overwhelmed by trauma. As Bucky became a "regular" on my rounds as a chaplain, it became evident that he had a gifting of being intuitive and discerning regarding the needs of others. He would rise beyond his normal, careful self and provide great comfort to patients.

Bucky had become a local hospital character, and we

began to notice doctors, nurses, staff, and patients all eager to have their "Bucky Time" cuddles.

One day while Bucky and I were doing visits in the trauma area, I was asked by the lead doctor to specifically visit a new head trauma patient. As we walked in, we could tell this young man was in pretty rough shape. Although his eyes seemed to light up when he saw Bucky, the young man was unable to do more than touch Bucky with a couple of fingers.

Mike had suffered severe head trauma from being beaten, which crushed his skull. Surgeons had to remove a section of his skull to allow for swelling and promote healing. I promised Bucky and I would be back in a week.

When we arrived the following Thursday, Mike (who had just gotten off the respirator) whispered loudly, "Can you get him up here?" I gently lifted Bucky's front feet onto his bed. This wasn't a new idea for Bucky, but he hadn't embraced the concept very well. But this time he seemed willing!

Mike said to Bucky, "You are so beautiful! Oh God, You made him so beautiful…I needed him in my life to give me hope. Thank You, God!"

Then I realized that Bucky was no longer just a few inches on the side of Mike's bed. Instead, my dog was leaning completely on the bed with only his back toes on the floor.

I said to Mike, "This is a first. Looks like Bucky wants to be in bed with you…Do you want me to get him down?"

Mike said, "No! Help him up here."

Soon Bucky and Mike were "cuddle buddies." Forty-five minutes later I took the smiling, cuddling Bucky from a smiling-but-exhausted Mike.

Later I got a call from a worker who told me Mike had been planning his own death as soon as he was released from the hospital. When I'd shared that Bucky was kind of nervous because he was recovering from being abused, Mike had decided that if God could heal and use Bucky that he should stop feeling sorry for himself for his problems and do like Bucky. Mike decided to find how he could help others instead.

We later ran into Mike when he had to come back to the hospital to get the removed section of his skull reattached. Mike and Bucky had an amazing reunion!

Who knew that a timid, young, nervous, eight-month-old pup would find a calling encouraging others who live through trauma too?[1]

Bucky was wounded and traumatized, and it impacted his personality. But out of his experiences, he'd developed a deep sensitivity and compassion. Now he helps others in ways that others can't. In God's plan and economy, no loss, crisis, or trauma is ever wasted. Perhaps you've experienced some trauma in your life. Because of that and what you've learned, you're in a unique position to help others. The apostle Paul wrote:

> Blessed be the God and Father of our Lord Jesus Christ, the Father of sympathy (pity and mercy) and the God [Who is the Source] of every comfort (consolation and encouragement), Who comforts (consoles and encourages) us in every trouble (calamity and affliction), so that we may also be able to comfort (console and encourage) those who are in any kind of trouble or distress, with the comfort (consolation and encouragement) with which we ourselves are comforted (consoled and encouraged) by God (2 Corinthians 1:3-4 AMP, brackets in original).

In what ways have you been comforted, consoled, and encouraged by God?

In what ways have you been comforted, consoled, and encouraged by others?

In what ways could you comfort, console, and encourage someone else?

Notes

Greetings

1. Max Lucado, *The Applause of Heaven* (Dallas: Word Publishing, 1990), 182. Used by permission.
2. Ibid., 183-84.
3. Ibid., 189-90.

The Master's Voice

1. Howard Macy, *Rhythms of Inner Life* (Colorado Springs: Chariot Victor, 1999), chapter 1.

The Nose Knows

1. Stanley Coren, *How Dogs Think* (New York: Free Press, 2004), adapted, 54-55. Used by permission.
2. David Baldacci, *Hell's Corner* (New York: Grand Central Publishing, 2010), 67.
3. Coren, *How Dogs Think*, 73. Used by permission.
4. Brad Steiger and Sharry Hansen Steiger, *Dog Miracles* (Avon, MA: Adams Media, 2001), adapted, 169.
5. Coren, *How Dogs Think*, 54-55. Used by permission.
6. Steiger and Steiger, *Dog Miracles*, adapted, 171.
7. Lloyd Ahlem, PhD, *Do I Have to Be Me?: The Psychology of Human Need* (Ventura, CA: Regal Books, 1973), 46-47.

Do Dogs Have Personality?

1. Bonnie Bergin, *Bonnie Bergin's Guide to Bringing Out the Best in Your Dog* (New York: Little, Brown & Co., 1995), 76.
2. Ibid., adapted, 73-77.
3. Ibid., adapted, 78.

Homing Instinct

1. Steiger and Steiger, *Dog Miracles*, adapted, 76-79. Used by permission.

You've Got to Be Kidding!

1. Brian Kilcommons and Sarah Wilson, *Tails from the Bark Side* (Boston: Warner Books, 1997), 44-48. Used by permission.
2. Charles Swindoll, *The Finishing Touch* (Dallas: Word Publishing, 1994), 220.

Change?

1. A.W. Tozer, *The Knowledge of the Holy* (New York: Harper Brothers, 1961), adapted, 61-62.

2. J.I. Packer, *Knowing God* (Downers Grove, IL: InterVarsity, 1973), adapted, 68-73.

Lost and Rescued

1. For more information, read Patricia Dibsie, *Love Heels* (New York: Yorkville Press, 2003).

Peace Is Possible!

1. John Ortberg, *Love Beyond Reason* (Grand Rapids, MI: Zondervan, 2001), 170.

2. Ibid., 170-71.

Up to No Good

1. Rebecca Currington, *Best Friends Forever—Me and My Dog: What I've Learned About Life, Love, and Faith from My Dog* (Grand Rapids, MI: Bethany House, 2010), 64-67. Used by permission.

How Close Are You?

1. Currington, *Best Friends Forever*, 52-55. Used by permission.

That Still Small Voice

1. Steiger and Steiger, *Dog Miracles*, adapted, 39-41. Used by permission.

The Wandering Dog

1. Currington, *Best Friends Forever*, 27.

2. H. Norman Wright, *A Better Way to Think* (Grand Rapids, MI: Revell, 2011), adapted, 87-88.

Ten Commandments: PART 1

1. Richard Lederer, *A Treasury for Dog Lovers* (New York: Howard Books, 2009), 42. Used by permission.

Ten Commandments: PART 2

1. Lederer, *Treasury for Dog Lovers*, 42. Used by permission.

Ten Commandments: PART 3

1. Lederer, *A Treasury for Dog Lovers*, 42-43. Used by permission.

Aging

1. Paula Payne Hardin, *What Are You Doing with the Rest of Your Life?* (San Rafael, CA: New World Library, 1992), adapted, 29-30.

2. Paul Tournier, *Learn to Grow Old* (London: SCM, 1971), 192.

3. Rob Moll, *The Art of Dying: Living Fully into the Life to Come* (Downers Grove, IL: IVP, 2010), 26.

4. Ken Gire, *The Reflective Life: Becoming More Spiritually Sensitive to the Everyday Moments of Life* (Colorado Springs: Chariot Victor, 1998), 85-86.

Saturated with the Word

1. H. Norman Wright, *What Men Want* (Ventura, CA: Regal Books, 1996), adapted, 158-61.

Loyalty and Faithfulness

1. Albert Peyson Terhune, *A Book of Famous Dogs* (New York: Triangle Books, 1914), adapted, 84-87.

The Word "Dog"

1. Author unknown, "Where Has My Little Dog Gone?" rhyme, circa 1860.

2. "Canary Islands," http://www.ctspanish.com/communities/canarym/canary%20islands.htm, accessed Feb. 1, 2013.

3. Lederer, *Treasury for Dog Lovers*, adapted, 5-17.

4. Answers: publicity hound; hushpuppies, put on the dog, dogleg, pup tent, dog days of summer, dog paddle.

Lost

1. Samson's story related to Norm Wright by Don and Billie.

2. Fritz's story related to Norm Wright by Martha.

The Touch of the Master

1. Linda Tellington Jones, *Getting in Touch with Your Dog* (North Pomfret, VT: Trafalgar Square Publishing, 2001), adapted, 58.

2. Ortberg, *Love Beyond Reason*, 56-58.

Your Pedigree

1. Lederer, *Treasury for Dog Lovers*, adapted, 73-77.

Guard Dog or Guard Your Dog?

1. Bergin, *Bonnie Bergin's Guide*, adapted, 30.

2. Gary Rosberg, *Guard Your Heart* (Sisters, OR: Multnomah, 1994), adapted, 15-17. Used by permission.

Earthquakes!

1. Stanley Coren, *How Dogs Think* (New York: Free Press, 2004), adapted, 111-18. Used by permission.

If You Believe This...

1. Will Rogers, "The Dog Who Paid Cash," *The Autobiography of Will Rogers* (New York: Houghton Mifflin Company, 1949). Used by permission.

2. Veronica Geng, "Canine Chateau," *Love Trouble Is My Business* (New York: HarperCollins Publishers, Inc., 1988). Used by permission.

Friendship

1. Patrick Morley, *The Man in the Mirror* (Brentwood, TN: Wolgemuth and Hyatt, 1989), 133.

2. Quoted in Garber, *Dog Love* (New York: Touchstone, 1997), as quoted in Jeffrey Moussaief Masson, *Dogs Never Lie About Love* (New York: Three Rivers Press, 1998), 4.

3. Jeffrey Moussaief Masson, *Dogs Never Lie About Love* (New York: Three Rivers Press, 1998), adapted, 4.

4. Voltaire, *Dictionaire philosopique*.

5. Cited in Helen and George Papashvily, *Dogs and People*, as quoted in Masson, *Dogs Never Lie About Love*, 11.

6. Masson, *Dogs Never Lie About Love*, 11

7. James Thurber, *Thurber's Dogs* (Whitby, ON: Fireside, 1992), 205-06.

8. Morley, *Man in the Mirror*, adapted, 135-36. Used by permission.

Do Dogs Worry?

1. John Haggai, *How to Win over Worry* (Eugene, OR: Harvest House Publishers, 1987), 16-17.

2. Gregory Jantz, *Overcoming Anxiety, Worry and Fear* (Grand Rapids, MI: Revell, 2011), 179.

Dancing Dogs

1. M.R. Wells, Kris Young, and Connie Fleishauer, *Paws for Reflection* (Eugene, OR: Harvest House Publishers, 2009), 45-46. Used by permission.

2. Ken Gire, *The Divine Embrace* (Carol Stream, IL: Tyndale House, 2003), 7-8. Used by permission.

Favorite Dog Stories

1. Jack London, *The Call of the Wild* (New York: Grosset & Dunlap, 1903), 150-51.

2. Ibid., 169-70.

3. Ibid., 173.

4. Dick Dickinson, paraphrase of 1 Corinthians 13:4-8, Inner Community Counseling Center, Long Beach, CA. Used by permission.

Growing Older

1. Lorry Lutz, *Looking Forward to the Rest of Your Life?: Embracing Midlife and Beyond* (Grand Rapids, MI: Baker Publishing Group, 2004), 73-78.

2. Tournier, *Learn to Grow Old,* 174-75.

3. Ibid., 210-11.

Tsunami Dog

1. Susy Flory, *Dog Tales* (Eugene, OR: Harvest House, 2011), adapted, 123-27. Used by permission.

How Do You Love?

1. David Teems, *And Thereby Hangs a Tale* (Eugene, OR: Harvest House, 2010), 153-54. Used by permission.

2. Ibid., 94-95. Used by permission.

3. Jack London, *White Fang* (1906), ch. 20.

4. William Shakespeare, *Romeo and Juliet*, Act II, Scene 1.

5. Jeffrey Masson, "Why We Cherish Dogs," 1997, www.nikkicraft.com/doggies/masson.html, accessed 5/22/2013.

6. Teems, *And Thereby Hangs a Tale*, 50-52. Used by permission.

What Do You Do?

1. Sporting group breed information taken from the AKC website, the Westminster Kennel Club website, and Petwave.com.

2. *Hi, It's Me, Your Dog* (Fresno, CA: Quill Driver Books, 2000), adapted, 28-38.

Dream On

1. Coren, *How Dogs Think*, 298-99.

2. Ibid., adapted, 297-99.

3. Michael Leuing, *A Common Prayer* (New York: HarperCollins, 1991). Used by permission.

Hidden or Found?

1. Gary Stanley, *What My Dog Has Taught Me About Life* (Colorado Springs: Honor Books, 2007), 120-22. Used by permission.

What If Your Dog Could Pray?

1. Herbert Brokering, *Dog Psalms* (Minneapolis: Augsburg Fortress, 2004), 14-15. Used by permission.

2. Ibid., 26-27.

Dog Truths or Myths?

1. Bergin, *Bonnie Bergin's Guide*, adapted, 47. Used by permission.

A Wounded Healer

1. Conversation between Major Ebel and Norm Wright. Used by permission.

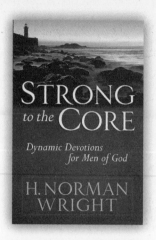

Strong to the Core

Strengthen Your Heart, Mind, and Spirit in Just 5 Minutes a Day

Bestselling author Norm Wright has a proven plan to help you strengthen your core—your spiritual life, your family life, and your personal life. In these short devotions you'll find biblical truth, wisdom for growing your relationships, and time-tested advice for handling temptations and working through problems.

Professional knowledge coupled with practical insights garnered through Norm's many years as a respected Christian counselor will help you...

- increase your understanding of the Lord and His will
- communicate more effectively in relationships, especially marriage
- strengthen your reliance on God and His Word
- develop traits that reveal your heart for God
- implement your faith and God-given gifts to help others

Strong to the Core encourages you to embrace God's call to live for Him, represent Him, and take a stand for Him. You can make a difference!

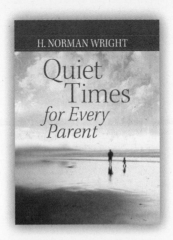

Quiet Times for Every Parent

Refreshing Moments with God

Parenthood is wonderful, but finding quiet times for yourself can seem impossible. It's not! Bestselling author and noted counselor Norm Wright provides encouragement, support, innovative ideas, and biblical wisdom in brief devotions to help you...

- encourage peace and joy at home
- know and provide what your children need
- grow in Christ even when days are hectic
- get revitalized when you're worn out
- cope on days when everything goes wrong

These short readings will provide an oasis filled with positive steps, uplifting hope, and moments of calm for your life as a busy parent.

Quiet Times for Couples

More than 550,000 copies sold!

*"Let Norman Wright guide you together to God...
and your marriage will never be the same."*
MAX LUCADO

Uplifting, insightful devotions that will inspire, encourage, and strengthen your marriage

In these short devotions that promote togetherness, joy, and sharing your dreams, trusted Christian counselor Norm Wright offers...

- innovative ideas to establish and maintain a flourishing marriage
- insights for encouraging intimacy and harmony
- little and big things you can do to enhance your relationship
- specific suggestions for accommodating differences and handling conflicts
- great ideas for supporting and helping your spouse

Your relationship will become more loving, considerate, and united as the two of you experience these quiet "together times" filled with deep insights, powerful meditations, God's presence, and His truths and love.